INVITATION TO ACTS

This volume continues a new series of commentaries specially designed to answer the need for a lively, contemporary guide to the written Word. Here is the best of contemporary biblical scholarship, together with the world-renowned Jerusalem Bible text. In addition, there are Study Questions that will provoke and inspire further reflection.

The Acts of the Apostles, written by the evangelist Luke, can be called the first history of the church after Christ's resurrection. First, it is an interpretive history of three major events facing the fledgling church: the destruction of Jerusalem, the difficulties that Christian missionaries were having, and the persecutions that were visited upon the followers of Christ. Acts is also the story of the lives of the earliest saints—Peter, the Twelve, Stephen, Philip, Barnabas, and, perhaps most influential of all, Paul, the apostle to the gentiles. It is in Acts that we learn of the lives and deaths of the leaders and their followers; of the heroism, both physical and spiritual, of the early church; of the life of Paul, who changed from greatest foe to greatest friend and ultimately martyr. And finally, Luke strives to be a pastor to the beleaguered faithful. He tries to make sense out of the problems of the present so the Christians can be ready for the future. It was a time of rapid change, and Luke reminds the early church of the continuity that can be found amid the seeming chaos.

Here is Luke's picture of life in the early church and in it can be seen the same kinds of problems that face the Christian of today. From it can be gotten the strength to remain believers in Jesus Christ in the face of almost insurmountable odds.

Invitation to Acts presents the Acts of the Apostles and its message in a format that can be easily used for individual study, daily meditation, and/or group discussion. It is an indispensable vo

D1501471

INVITATION TO ACTS

*A Commentary on the Acts of the Apostles with
Complete Text from The Jerusalem Bible*

ROBERT J. KARRIS

IMAGE BOOKS
A Division of Doubleday & Company, Inc.
Garden City, New York
1978

For Russ and Sammy

The text of the Acts of the Apostles is from The Jerusalem Bible,
Copyright © 1966 by Darton, Longman & Todd, Ltd., and Doubleday & Company, Inc. Used by permission of the publisher.

ISBN: 0-385-12210-1
Library of Congress Catalog Card Number: 77-91558
Commentary Copyright © 1978 by Robert J. Karris
General Introduction Copyright © 1977 by Robert J. Karris
All Rights Reserved
Printed in the United States of America
First Edition

CONTENTS

ABBREVIATIONS OF THE BOOKS
OF THE BIBLE

Ac	Acts	Lk	Luke
Am	Amos	Lm	Lamentations
Ba	Baruch	Lv	Leviticus
1 Ch	1 Chronicles	1 M	1 Maccabees
2 Ch	2 Chronicles	2 M	2 Maccabees
1 Co	1 Corinthians	Mi	Micah
2 Co	2 Corinthians	Mk	Mark
Col	Colossians	Ml	Malachi
Dn	Daniel	Mt	Matthew
Dt	Deuteronomy	Na	Nahum
Ep	Ephesians	Nb	Numbers
Est	Esther	Ne	Nehemiah
Ex	Exodus	Ob	Obadiah
Ezk	Ezekiel	1 P	1 Peter
Ezr	Ezra	2 P	2 Peter
Ga	Galatians	Ph	Philippians
Gn	Genesis	Phm	Philemon
Hab	Habakkuk	Pr	Proverbs
Heb	Hebrews	Ps	Psalms
Hg	Haggai	Qo	Ecclesiastes
Ho	Hosea	Rm	Romans
Is	Isaiah	Rt	Ruth
Jb	Job	Rv	Revelation
Jdt	Judith	1 S	1 Samuel
Jg	Judges	2 S	2 Samuel
Jl	Joel	Sg	Song of Songs
Jm	James	Si	Ecclesiasticus
Jn	John	Tb	Tobit
1 Jn	1 John	1 Th	1 Thessalonians
2 Jn	2 John	2 Th	2 Thessalonians
3 Jn	3 John	1 Tm	1 Timothy
Jon	Jonah	2 Tm	2 Timothy
Jos	Joshua	Tt	Titus
Jr	Jeremiah	Ws	Wisdom
Jude	Jude	Zc	Zechariah
1 K	1 Kings	Zp	Zephaniah
2 K	2 Kings		

GENERAL INTRODUCTION TO
THE DOUBLEDAY NEW TESTAMENT
COMMENTARY SERIES

Let me introduce this new commentary series on the New Testament by sharing some experiences. In my job as New Testament Book Review Editor for the *Catholic Biblical Quarterly,* scores of books pass through my hands each year. As I evaluate these books and send them out to reviewers, I cannot help but think that so little of this scholarly research will make its way into the hands of the educated lay person.

In talking at biblical institutes and to charismatic and lay study groups, I find an almost unquenchable thirst for the Word of God. People want to learn more; they want to study. But when they ask me to recommend commentaries on the New Testament, I'm stumped. What commentaries can I put into their hands, commentaries that do not have the technical jargon of scholars and that really communicate to the educated laity?

The goal of this popular commentary series is to make the best of contemporary scholarship available to the educated lay person in a highly readable and understandable way. The commentaries avoid footnotes and other scholarly apparatus. They are short and sweet. The authors make their points in a clear way and don't fatigue their readers with unnecessary detail.

Another outstanding feature of this commentary series is that it is based on The Jerusalem Bible translation, which is serialized with the commentary. This lively and easily understandable translation has received rave reviews from millions of readers. It is the interstate of translations and avoids the stoplights of local-road translations.

A signal feature of these commentaries is that they explore the way each biblical author met the needs of his church. The commentators answer the question: How did each author guide, challenge, teach, and console the members of his community? The commentators are not interested in the author's message for its own sake, but explain that message with one eye on present application.

This last-mentioned feature goes hand and glove with the innovative feature of appending Study Questions to the explanations of individual passages. By means of these Study Questions the commentator moves from an explanation of the message of the biblical author to a consideration of how this message might apply to believers today.

Each commentator has two highly important qualifications: scholarly expertise and the proven ability to communicate the results of solid scholarship to the people of God.

I am confident that this new commentary series will meet a real need as it helps people to unlock a door to the storehouse of God's Word where they will find food for life.

ROBERT J. KARRIS, O.F.M.
Associate Professor of New Testament Studies,
Catholic Theological Union and
Chicago Cluster of Theological Schools

INTRODUCTION

Let me begin this Introduction by inviting you to engage in a game of free association of ideas. When I say "The Acts of the Apostles," what idea do you immediately associate with it? I would bet that the first idea that came to your mind was something like "*History* of the early church." Concluding our brief game, I ask, "But what is history?"

IS HISTORY A DESCRIPTION OF WHAT ACTUALLY HAPPENED?

Suppose you read three newspaper accounts of the same event. In one newspaper the bald facts are chronicled: "This afternoon, after three months' work, the wrecking ball completed the demolition of the Stock Exchange Building. Next week construction will begin on the forty-story KFX Building." In another newspaper you read that "with the silencing of the wrecking ball the city has moved out of the nineteenth century into the twentieth. An old, inefficient building no longer takes up valuable space. Progress is the keyword. The KFX Building will inspire a wave of new, modernistic, efficient skyscrapers which will pour millions of tax dollars into the city coffers." A third newspaper grieves over the destruction of the Stock Exchange Building and prints this obituary: "Today this city's love for beauty and grandeur died. The city fathers killed a landmark and plan to replace it with a steel and concrete monstrosity. They sold beauty into bondage for a pottage of tax dollars." Which of these three accounts captures the real meaning of the event?

Is the mere chronicling of an event history? Can there be historical writing without interpretation?

THE ACTS OF THE APOSTLES IS BIBLICAL HISTORY

For the historical writers of the Old Testament, in whose tradition Luke stands, there was no such thing as the mere chronicling of events. Events were interpreted—just as the event of the demolition of the Stock Exchange Building was interpreted. As an example of this type of history writing, let us take the account which the author of 1 Kings gives of King Solomon's last days:

> When Solomon grew old his wives swayed his heart to other gods; and his heart was not wholly with Yahweh his God as his father David's had been. . . . Yahweh therefore said to Solomon, 'Since you behave like this and do not keep my covenant or the laws I laid down for you, I will most surely tear the kingdom away from you and give it to one of your servants. For your father David's sake, however, I will not do this during your lifetime, but will tear it out of your son's hands. Even so, I will not tear the whole kingdom from him. For the sake of my servant David, and for the sake of Jerusalem which I have chosen, I will leave your son one tribe.' . . . The rest of the history of Solomon, his entire career, his wisdom, is not all this recorded in the Book of the Acts of Solomon? Solomon's reign in Jerusalem over all Israel lasted forty years. Then Solomon slept with his ancestors and was buried in the Citadel of David his father; Rehoboam his son succeeded him. [1 K 11:4, 11–13, 41–43]

As the narrative itself says, Solomon did many other things during the last years of his reign. But the author of 1 Kings is concerned only about one phase of those activities—Solomon's idolatry. All of Solomon's accomplishments pale in the face of this fact. Yet Yahweh is merciful because of his promise to David.

Why did the author of 1 Kings interpret Solomon's life this way? The author is writing his "history" to edify the Jewish people after the Babylonian Exile. This portion of the story of Solomon warns them of what will be in store for them if they do not truly repent and faithfully obey Yahweh's commandments. This story also inspires hope in them and gives them encouragement, for Yahweh is faithful to his promises. Yahweh did not annihilate his people, but rescued them because of his fidelity to his promises.

LUKE'S HISTORY INTERPRETS KEY EVENTS OF HIS TIME

Luke's writing of the Acts of the Apostles can be likened to the writing of the history of Solomon found in 1 Kings. It can also be likened to the interpretation of the event of the razing of the Stock Exchange Building. As the various sections of the commentary will make clear, Luke writes to interpret three major events which agitate his missionary communities. One of these events is the destruction of Jerusalem. This event, Luke says, does not mean that God has not been faithful to his promises. Just as the Babylonian Exile did not signal an end to God's fidelity, so too the destruction of Jerusalem and its Temple does not mean that God will not honor his promises. In Acts Luke goes out of his way to demonstrate that the God whom the Christians worship can be called God-faithful-to-promises. For example, God has not abandoned the suffering righteous

one, Jesus, who was martyred, but has given him the
life of the resurrection.

Part and parcel of Luke's stress on God's fidelity to
his promises is his view of God's will and purpose.
Whatever happens for Luke's communities happens according to God's will and purpose. God is leading his
community; he it is who directs them to undertake a
mission to the pagans. He it is who calls Paul and turns
this fierce persecutor of the church into the greatest
missionary the primitive church knew.

Another major event confronting Luke's missionary
communities was the difficulty of mission. Some Jews
were converted, but many refused to believe that Jesus
was the fulfillment of God's promises. In this trying situation some Christians were tempted to say that the
Lord had abandoned his missionaries, that he was absent. To allay this temptation, Luke stresses that the
Lord Jesus is present in his Name and Spirit. By the
power of that Name and Spirit the Christian mission
continues and will be successful. The Acts of the Apostles also provides Luke's missionaries to the Jews with
strong apologetic arguments. The Twelve stand in continuity with Jesus, who is God's fulfillment of his promises. These Twelve, who symbolize the twelve patriarchs as shepherds of the twelve tribes of Israel, win
thousands of repentant Jews to Jesus with their preaching in Jerusalem. These form the restored Israel. Paul,
who stands in the best tradition of Judaism, continues
the preaching of God's Word to Jew and pagan despite
almost insuperable odds. And the Roman authorities,
before whom Paul is accused by the Jews, pronounce
him innocent. Just as Jesus and Paul did not abandon
missionary work despite grievous opposition from the
Jews, so too Luke's missionaries should not (see Lk
10:1–24 and Ac 13:1 to 28:31).

A final situation within Luke's community which

prompted him to write his history was persecution from
Jews and pagans. Luke has multiple lessons of consolation for his persecuted people. Just as Jesus, the
founder of the Christian Way, was persecuted and martyred, so too does his community suffer persecution. In
Acts, Luke stresses that persecution is not continuous.
God does rescue his own from persecution. Even
though Jesus' missionaries may be martyred like Stephen was, they should imitate Jesus, who forgave his
persecutors and committed his soul to his Father. Jesus
does not allow death to spit in the faces of those who
shed their blood for him and his Word. His martyrs are
honored with union with him to whom they have been
faithful. Lastly, Luke shows his communities that persecution leads to the spread of the Word. From persecution and death comes growth.

LUKE WRITES HISTORY TO EDIFY

Like the author of 1 Kings, Luke writes history to
edify. In a situation of perplexity and strain, Luke challenges his missionary communities to take a profound
and long look at their history. That history contains the
seeds of life for the present. From what they can garner
from their contemplation of the past, Luke's communities can meaningfully scan the horizons of the future. In
a nutshell, Luke writes history so that his communities
can make sense out of their present. From their appreciation of the present they will know how to respond to
the future.

THE ACTS OF THE APOSTLES IS ALSO HAGI-
OGRAPHY

I apologize for using the twenty-five-dollar word
hagiography. But this technical word aptly captures an-

other aspect of what Luke is about in the Acts of the
Apostles. He is engaged in hagiography: that is, he is
writing a book about the lives of the saints. Peter, the
Twelve, Stephen, Philip, Barnabas, and Paul are the
saints about whom Luke writes.

In order to prime the pump for an appreciation of
Luke, the first Christian hagiographer, let's cite some
examples from the hagiography of a very popular saint
—Francis of Assisi. Thomas of Celano, St. Francis of
Assisi's first "biographer," has these two provocative
descriptions of Francis:

> The people would offer Francis bread to
> bless, which they would then keep for a long
> time; and, upon eating it, they were cured of
> various illnesses. So also they very often cut off
> parts of his tunic in their very great faith, so
> much so that he sometimes was left almost
> naked. And what is even more wonderful, if the
> holy father would touch any object with his
> hand, health returned to many by means of that
> object. [*First Life,* 63]

> And because he always bore and preserved
> Christ Jesus and him crucified in his heart with
> a wonderful love, he was marked in a most
> glorious way above all others with the seal of
> him whom in a rapture of mind he contem-
> plated. . . . [*First Life,* 115]

To show how near Francis was to God, his biographer
uses a literary form and describes him as performing
wonders and marvels. In the second example, Thomas
of Celano waxes eloquent on the fact that Francis bore
in his hands, feet, and side the wounds of Christ—the
stigmata. The stigmata made Francis' *imitation of*

Christ complete. With these two examples of hagiography in mind, let us examine the Acts of the Apostles.

THE SPIRIT-FILLED PETER AND PAUL IMITATE THE SPIRIT-FILLED JESUS

For Luke, Jesus is the man of the Spirit par excellence. His entire life was lived in communion with God's Spirit. Those who stand in continuity with him are united to the same Spirit. Pentecost celebrates that gift of the Spirit. Peter and Paul are men of the Spirit. The Spirit impels them to mission, to continue Jesus' work of performing miracles to restore people to the wholeness promised by God in the Old Testament. Luke spotlights how Paul imitates and follows in the footsteps of the martyr Jesus (see the commentaries on 19:1 to 28:31).

But Luke does not depict Peter and Paul as Spirit-filled men merely to show how they imitate Jesus. He is setting up models for his missionaries. Just as Thomas of Celano sets up Francis of Assisi as a model Christian, so too does Luke set up Peter and Paul as models for the Christians of his own day.

HAGIOGRAPHY, THE MIRACULOUS, AND HUMOR

The story quoted above of Francis of Assisi's miracle-working abilities is similar to some descriptions in the Acts of the Apostles. Prison doors fly open, angels come and go, shadows and handkerchiefs cure. To the popular mind a saint performs stupendous miracles.

The popular mind also delights in the humorous. With a smile dancing along his lips, Thomas of Celano

tells about Francis being stripped almost naked by folk
intent on clipping off pieces of his miracle-working
tunic. In many places Luke entertains his readers with
similar humor. For example, in 19:15–16 he has the
evil spirit turn against Jewish exorcists who tried to
mimic Paul: "The evil spirit replied, 'Jesus I recognize,
and I know who Paul is, but who are you?' and the
man with the evil spirit hurled himself at them and
overpowered first one and then another, and handled
them so violently that they fled from that house naked
and badly mauled."

LUKE THE PASTOR AND US

We have talked about Luke the history-writer and
the hagiographer. We have hinted at his motivation for
donning these two hats—he wants to edify his missionary communities. At this point, I want to summon
Luke back on stage and applaud him for his role as the
pastor who excels in edifying his audience.

One of Luke's most precious gifts to the church is
his view of Jesus and the Spirit—they are for mission.
Jesus and the Spirit are not solely for the individual
Christian. They lavish gifts upon Christians so that they
might use these gifts for others. Luke shares with his
readers and us the profound truth that Jesus would not
be Messiah if his church did not engage in missionary
work. (As a matter of fact, some commentators maintain that Luke's purpose in writing a sequel to his Gospel was to expound this profound truth.) The Spirit is
not busy bestowing "warm fuzzies" on individual Christians so that they can feel snug and smug. In Acts the
Spirit compels and impels Christians to mission.

Jesus and Paul did not have an easy time of it.
Christian missionaries should take note. There is going

to be persecution. But all is not black and bleak. There are the sterling examples of Peter and Paul, of Stephen and Barnabas. There is the support of one's missionary companions, the support of the mission-sending community, and most importantly the support of God in prayer. It is not happenstance that prayer plays such an important role in Acts. Prayer opens up the channels of communication between God and his church, so that the missionaries can know and act according to God's will and purpose.

In their missionary activity the Christian church will constantly struggle in a search for continuity amidst discontinuity. For example, how much of the Jewish heritage are pagans required to assimilate into their lives when they become Christians? Must they be circumcised? What happens when a Christian message, developed in a parochial setting, moves into a cosmopolitan city like Antioch? Will the missionaries, for example, have to tone down their message of concern for the poor in the face of a culture which shows little concern for them? In this era of rapid change in all churches, Luke's quest for continuity amidst discontinuity strikes a resonant chord.

In detailing the fine qualities of Luke the pastor, we may have given the impression that he sees himself as a problem-solver, that he has eyes for nothing but problems within his community. To a large extent Luke is a problem-solver, because life generates problems. But there is also a vast other side to Luke's abilities as a pastor. He is an optimist, a man of vision. His picture of the early days of the Jerusalem community in Acts 2:41–47 and 4:31–35 may be idyllic and ideal. But it is not false. Luke holds up an ideal which challenges his communities and us. An ideal, a vision, forces us to stretch our imaginations, to exceed our low expectations of ourselves, not to be satisfied with mediocrity.

We might turn our backs on Luke's ideal, but it is not false.

Luke not only presents the ideal of a community at prayer, celebrating fellowship, and enjoying the breaking of bread; he also projects a very positive view of God. God is merciful, loving, and faithful. All three characteristics mingle together in Luke's picture of God-faithful-to-promises. That is who God is. Because God has been faithful to his promises in the past, we trust that he will be faithful to us in the present. And because God is such a rock, such a pillar, such a mainstay, we can begin to discern his will for us in the present. And because of our faith and hope in God's trustworthiness we can walk with confidence into the future he has prepared for us.

Yes, Luke is an excellent pastor. With empathy and brilliance he solves the problems of his communities and of future generations. But his most important contribution to the church is his vision of who God is and what the church should be.

(The reader can profitably consult the Introduction of *Invitation to Luke* for more details on what Luke was about in his two-volume work.)

ACKNOWLEDGMENTS

It is my pleasant task to single out three individuals for special praise and thanks. I have learned much from the outstanding commentary on Acts by the late Ernst Haenchen. Robert T. Heller, my editorial director at Doubleday, has been of benefit to me and this commentary series in many ways. I thank him for his vision, encouragement, and understanding. Ms. Shirley Brin has been a steady support to me and my work as she has expertly prepared this manuscript for publication. I thank her for her support and assistance.

The Beginnings of Mission
Acts 1:1 to 2:13

Acts 1:1–11
HAVE CONFIDENCE IN YOUR ASCENDED LORD

1 In my earlier work, Theophilus, I dealt with everything Jesus had done and taught from the ² beginning ·until the day he gave his instructions to the apostles he had chosen through the Holy ³ Spirit, and was taken up to heaven. ·He had shown himself alive to them after his Passion by many demonstrations: for forty days he had continued to appear to them and tell them about the king- ⁴ dom of God. ·When he had been at table with them, he had told them not to leave Jerusalem, but to wait there for what the Father had prom- ised. "It is," he had said, "what you have heard ⁵ me speak about: ·John baptized with water but you, not many days from now, will be baptized with the Holy Spirit."

⁶ Now having met together, they asked him, "Lord, has the time come? Are you going to ⁷ restore the kingdom to Israel?" ·He replied, "It is not for you to know times or dates that the Father ⁸ has decided by his own authority, ·but you will receive power when the Holy Spirit comes on you, and then you will be my witnesses not only in Jerusalem but throughout Judaea and Samaria, and indeed to the ends of the earth."

⁹ As he said this he was lifted up while they looked on, and a cloud took him from their sight. ¹⁰ They were still staring into the sky when suddenly ¹¹ two men in white were standing near them ·and they said, "Why are you men from Galilee stand- ing here looking into the sky? Jesus who has been taken up from you into heaven, this same Jesus will come back in the same way as you have seen him go there."

✠

In this introduction Luke relates Acts to his first volume, the Gospel (1:1–2), and gives voice to the themes which will sound through his second volume (1:3–11).

Before we elucidate Luke's themes, however, a serious problem claims our attention. This section boasts an account of Jesus' ascension which is inconsistent with the one found in Luke 24:50–53. In Acts 1:1–11 Jesus ascends forty days after his resurrection, whereas in Luke 24:50–53 he ascends on the day of his resurrection. This problem of inconsistency partially evaporates if we view Luke as a historian in the finest Old Testament tradition. He does not strive for tape-recorder accuracy, but thrives on showing how God's will directed, and was manifested in, the course of events. We can solve the remainder of the problem of inconsistency by observing that Luke often uses multiple accounts of the same event to focus attention on different aspects of the rich tapestry of that event (see, e.g., the three accounts of Paul's call in 9:1–19; 22:1–21; 26:1–23). In the Gospel the ascension, not the resurrection, concludes the gospel story and signals the lordship of the Jesus who is worshiped by the apostles (Lk 24:52). In Acts Jesus ascends so that as Lord he can fulfill his promises of the gift of the Spirit and of the spread of the Word to the ends of the earth (Ac 1:8).

Luke gives voice to two major themes in this section: (1) fulfillment of promise; (2) continuity between Jesus and his community. The theme of fulfillment of promise operates on a number of levels. First, in verse 8 Jesus gives a mandate which is also a promise. The story of Acts will detail how that promise is fulfilled at Pentecost and then in the mission in

Jerusalem, throughout Judaea (chapters 1 to 7), in Samaria (chapters 8 and 9), and to the ends of the earth (chapters 10 to 28). One could say that Acts is an account of how Jesus was faithful to the promise he gave in 1:8.

Another level on which the theme of fulfillment of promise functions appears in Luke's interpretation of the Old Testament promises in such a way that Jesus would not be Messiah unless he founded a missionary community (see Ac 1:8). This understanding of the meaning of Jesus the Messiah is present in Luke 24:46–47, but is expressed most clearly in Paul's defense before King Agrippa: "But I was blessed with God's help, and so I have stood firm to this day, testifying to great and small alike, saying nothing more than what the prophets and Moses himself said would happen: that the Christ was to suffer and that, as the first to rise from the dead, *he was to proclaim that light now shone for our people and for the pagans too*" (Ac 26:22–23). The only way that Jesus, after his death and resurrection, can proclaim light for both Jew and gentile is through the preaching of his missionary community. Seen from this perspective, Acts is the edifying story of how Jesus, through the mission of his community, is the Messiah who fulfills the Old Testament promise that the Messiah's light will shine for both Jew and gentile.

Luke's concern with the theme of fulfillment of promise operates on yet a third level. Luke does not construct a theology of fulfillment of promise in ivory-tower serenity. He fashions his theology to exhort his persecuted, missionary community to have greater confidence in its Lord. Luke's community, as it reflects on the narration in Acts of how the Lord's promises were fulfilled, can draw consolation that the Lord is faithful and will honor the promises he has made to them. In its trials which stem from persecution and from the poor response Jews and gentiles have given to its preaching, the community should not be despondent and challenge: "Lord, has the time come? Are you going to restore the kingdom to Israel?" (1:6). Luke's answer is the perplexing but assuring word: It is not for you to know the times, but to believe that I am faithful to my promises (see 1:7–8). Despite indications to the contrary, Jesus is truly Lord and faithfully cares for his people.

In sum, through the theme of fulfillment of promise Luke encourages his harassed, missionary community that Jesus is Messiah and Lord for them.

The second prominent theme in this section is that the apostles provide the link between Jesus and his community. Luke narrates no appearances of the resurrected Lord in Galilee. Jesus appears to the apostles in Jerusalem, that symbol of God's fidelity to his people and promises. Jesus gives further instructions to his apostles about the kingdom of God (1:3), which was the hallmark of his preaching and is to be that of his apostles. Jesus' last words on earth are addressed to his apostles, and are a command to be his witnesses (1:8). They, men from Galilee (1:11), can be his witnesses because they have seen and heard what he had done and taught from the beginning (1:1; and cf. especially 1:21–22).

STUDY QUESTIONS: Who is our source of continuity with Jesus? Can today's troubled church draw inspiration and encouragement from the fact that Jesus has been faithful to his promises in the past?

Acts 1:12–26
THE RECIPIENTS OF THE
PROMISED HOLY SPIRIT

12 So from the Mount of Olives, as it is called, they went back to Jerusalem, a short distance away, no
13 more than a sabbath walk; ·and when they reached the city they went to the upper room where they were staying; there were Peter and John, James and Andrew, Philip and Thomas, Bartholomew and Matthew, James son of Alphaeus and Simon the Zealot, and Jude son of
14 James. ·All these joined in continuous prayer, together with several women, including Mary the mother of Jesus, and with his brothers.

15 One day Peter stood up to speak to the brothers —there were about a hundred and twenty persons
16 in the congregation: ·"Brothers, the passage of scripture had to be fulfilled in which the Holy Spirit, speaking through David, foretells the fate of Judas, who offered himself as a guide to the
17 men who arrested Jesus—·after having been one of our number and actually sharing this ministry of
18 ours. ·As you know, he bought a field with the money he was paid for his crime. He fell headlong and burst open, and all his entrails poured out.
19 Everybody in Jerusalem heard about it and the field came to be called the Bloody Acre, in their
20 language Hakeldama. ·Now in the Book of Psalms it says:

> Let his camp be reduced to ruin,
> Let there be no one to live in it.

And again:

> Let someone else take his office.

21 "We must therefore choose someone who has been with us the whole time that the Lord Jesus
22 was traveling around with us, ·someone who was with us right from the time when John was baptizing until the day when he was taken up from us— and he can act with us as a witness to his resurrection."
23 Having nominated two candidates, Joseph known as Barsabbas, whose surname was Justus,
24 and Matthias, ·they prayed, "Lord, you can read everyone's heart; show us therefore which of these
25 two you have chosen ·to take over this ministry and apostolate which Judas abandoned to go to
26 his proper place." ·They then drew lots for them, and as the lot fell to Matthias, he was listed as one of the twelve apostles.

☩

If Acts is the story of how the promise Jesus made in 1:8 is fulfilled, we might very well ask: Is Luke a good storyteller? One who tells a story vividly and with clarity? Or one who meanders and loses the reader? This section could easily give the impression that Luke does not tell a good story. The promise given in 1:8 leads the reader to expect that the next event to be narrated would be the coming of the Holy Spirit. But 1:15–26 seems to be nothing but a meandering which adds nothing to the development of the story of Acts; as a matter of fact, Matthias, the new apostle (1:26), nowhere else figures in the story of Acts. Why didn't Luke proceed immediately from 1:11 to 2:1 and narrate the event of Pentecost? He didn't because he first had to tell his readers about the three groups who would receive the Holy Spirit.

The first group is the apostles, who return to Jerusalem, God's chosen city (1:12). Their names are given in 1:13. These names, with Peter's in the position of prominence, are the same as those found in Lk

6:14–16—except Judas. Verses 15–26 are concerned with the selection of a replacement for Judas. Peter's speech (1:16–22), like the other speeches in Acts, is directed toward Luke's Greek-speaking audience. That's the most likely explanation for the two incongruities found in the speech: (1) Peter tells his listeners a story which they presumably already know; (2) Peter's quotation of Psalm 69:25 in the first part of verse 20 makes sense only if Peter presumes the Greek translation of the psalm; the Hebrew has "*their* camp" rather than "his camp." Through Peter's speech Luke employs his theology of fulfillment of promise to show his readers why Judas *had to come* (1:16) to such a gruesome fate and why someone else *must be* chosen to replace him (1:21). Put another way, through Peter's speech Luke is telling his readers that the number of *twelve* apostles must be filled up before the Holy Spirit can be given. There are two reasons for this. First, there is need, as verses 21–22 so clearly delineate, for another witness of what Jesus did and said during his ministry, another witness to Jesus' resurrection (see Ac 1:1–2 and Lk 1:1–4). These apostolic witnesses will provide the link between Jesus and the Christian community. (Incidentally, according to the definition of an apostle given in 1:21–22, Paul cannot be an apostle, for he had not been a witness to the earthly life of Jesus. For Luke there are only twelve apostles; but see Ac 14:4, 14.) Secondly, since Israel's restoration was pictured through the image of the restoration of the twelve patriarchs, the twelve apostles symbolize the reconstituted Israel. The completion of the number of *twelve* apostles indicates that those who will receive the promised Holy Spirit are the integral, restored Israel, heirs to all God's promises.

Verse 14 pinpoints the second group present at Pentecost: "together with several women, including Mary the mother of Jesus, and with his brothers." Why these people? They provide additional links between Jesus and the community and are representative of the attitudes needed to receive the gift of the Holy Spirit (see how Luke begins his first volume in a similar way in Lk 1:5 to 2:52 with the stories of people like Mary, Simeon, and Anna, who are open to God's revelation). The women are those faithful followers of Jesus (see Lk 8:1–3) who remained with him steadfastly to the end (Lk 23:49, 55–56; 24:9–11). Mary, the mother of Jesus, and his brothers are mentioned because they are disciples of Jesus and examples of those who heard the Word of God and did it (see Lk 8:19–21). Mary is also a witness of Jesus' infancy.

The third group is singled out in verse 15, where it is simply said, without any explanation, that Peter is in charge of the *120*. The number 120 points to the establishment of a new community, for rabbinic law as formulated in the Mishnah (Sanhedrin 1:6) stated that 120 inhabitants were needed before a town could have a small sanhedrin.

As we will have frequent opportunity to note, Luke is a fine storyteller. But sometimes, as in this section, he makes his point in what might seem a roundabout way. Those who await the gift of the Holy Spirit are twelve apostles who represent restored Israel; women, Mary, and Jesus' brothers who represent steadfast discipleship; and 120 brethren who represent a new community.

Finally, not only do verses 12–26 describe who the recipients of the gift of the Holy Spirit are, but they also narrate how they prepared for that gift—in continuous prayer (1:14). As he had done in his first volume (see, e.g., Lk 18:1–8), Luke emphasizes the importance of prayer. On the significance of prayer in Acts, see, for example 10:9, 30, and 11:5—prayer be-

fore God calls the first gentile, Cornelius—and 22:17—
prayer before God sends Paul on mission to the gentiles.

STUDY QUESTIONS: In what sense does prayer prepare
a person for God's gifts? Does
Luke so emphasize God's direction
of history, as evidenced in Judas'
demise (1:16) and the necessity of
choosing a replacement (1:21),
that he leaves little room for the exercise of free will?

Acts 2:1–13
SPIRIT AND MISSION

¹ ² 2 When Pentecost day came around, they had all met in one room, ·when suddenly they heard what sounded like a powerful wind from heaven, the noise of which filled the entire house ³ in which they were sitting; ·and something appeared to them that seemed like tongues of fire; these separated and came to rest on the head of ⁴ each of them. ·They were all filled with the Holy Spirit, and began to speak foreign languages as the Spirit gave them the gift of speech.

⁵ Now there were devout men living in Jerusalem ⁶ from every nation under heaven, ·and at this sound they all assembled, each one bewildered to ⁷ hear these men speaking his own language. ·They were amazed and astonished. "Surely," they said, ⁸ "all these men speaking are Galileans? ·How does it happen that each of us hears them in his own ⁹ native language? ·Parthians, Medes and Elamites; people from Mesopotamia, Judaea and Cappa- ¹⁰ docia, Pontus and Asia, ·Phrygia and Pamphylia, Egypt and the parts of Libya around Cyrene; as ¹¹ well as visitors from Rome—·Jews and proselytes alike—Cretans and Arabs; we hear them preaching in our own language about the marvels of God." ¹² Everyone was amazed and unable to explain it; ¹³ they asked one another what it all meant. ·Some, however, laughed it off. "They have been drinking too much new wine," they said.

✠

Exploring this passage is like viewing a brilliant sun-set. Colors crowd in upon one another with such rapidity, leaping across the length of the spectrum, exploding, and dissipating, that it is difficult to secure a vantage point from which to appreciate the beauty of the sunset in its entirety. Let's try to capture the beauty of this passage by taking seven high-speed color photos from different angles.

First, what happens at Pentecost is the fulfillment of the promise of 1:4–5, 8 (see also 2:33). But, as is most often the case in Luke's presentation, the fulfillment does not stamp "Finished" on a promise. Rather the fulfillment contains within itself the seeds of a new promise. In the case at hand, this new promise is that the Spirit will guide the community's mission. Fulfillments of that promise are traced in passages such as 10:19–20; 11:12; 13:4; 16:6–7; 19:21; 20:22.

Second, the Spirit's coming, an interior experience, is described exteriorly "like a powerful wind from heaven" and "like tongues of fire." What's behind these symbols of wind and fire? In Jewish tradition wind and fire are symbols of God's presence. For example Psalm 50:3 has: "Let our God come, and be silent no more! Preceding him, a devouring *fire,* around him, a raging storm" (see also Is 66:15). In this instance the Lord is present in fire and wind for judgment. The Jewish tradition which approximates our passage most closely is one found in the writings of Philo, an Alexandrian Jew of about A.D. 50, who describes God's supreme revelation on Sinai with the symbols of fire and sound: "Then from the midst of the fire that streamed from heaven there sounded forth to their utter amazement a voice, for the flame became articulate speech in the language familiar to the audience, and so clearly and distinctly were the words formed by it that they seemed to see rather than hear them" (*On the Decalogue,* 46; Loeb translation). "The marvels of God" (2:11), preached on Pentecost, are like the ten commandments, for both stem from God as the symbols of wind and *tongues* of fire indicate.

Third, the coming of the Holy Spirit is also symbolized exteriorly in this passage with the term "language" (2:4, 6, 11; a more literal translation would be "tongue"). As in 1 Corinthians 14:2 and especially in Acts 10:44–47 and 19:6, the coming of the Holy Spirit is externally visible because the recipients speak in tongues (languages).

Fourth, although it is clear that "all" (2:1, 4— presumably meaning the 120, the women, Mary, and Jesus' brothers) receive the Holy Spirit, yet only the twelve apostles are singled out in 2:8 and 14. While the twelve apostles are most important for Luke's presentation of the spread of the mission, he also preserves the notion that the Holy Spirit was given to a larger group. Could he be heir to a tradition similar to that enshrined in 1 Corinthians 15:5–6, wherein mention is first made of an appearance of the Risen Lord to the Twelve and then to a larger group of five hundred? That Luke is aware of a larger group of recipients is again clear in 2:17–18, which details both men and women as recipients of the Spirit.

Fifth, as the list of who's who in the world reveals (2:9–11), the Spirit's coming has meaning for all peoples.

Sixth, there is some linguistic evidence that in 2:6 ("each one *bewildered* to hear these men *speaking his own language*") there is an allusion to the reversal of the event of Babel described in Genesis 11:7: "Come, let us go down and *confuse their language* on the spot so that they can no longer understand one another." Through the gift of the Holy Spirit all nations will be able to understand the message of the Risen Lord.

Seventh, Pentecost, the harvest feast (see Lv 23:15–16), is singled out because it seems to have been the actual day on which the primitive community experienced the gift of the Holy Spirit which impelled them to mission to all people.

Through these seven observations we have attempted to capture some of the power and the beauty of Luke's account of the reception of the Holy Spirit. This powerful experience can be articulated as follows: When the Holy Spirit impels the community to mission, the word it preaches is the Lord's.

STUDY QUESTIONS: Do we find new Pentecosts in the church today? Is the gift of the Spirit reserved to any special category of people within the church? Do our pictorial representations of Pentecost do justice to the meaning of the event?

The Mission in Jerusalem and Judaea
Acts 2:14 to 8:3

Acts 2:14–41
PENTECOST INTERPRETED

¹⁴ Then Peter stood up with the Eleven and addressed them in a loud voice:

"Men of Judaea, and all you who live in Jerusalem, make no mistake about this, but listen carefully to what I say. ·These men are not drunk, as you imagine; why, it is only the third hour of the day. ·On the contrary, this is what the prophet spoke of:

¹⁷ In the days to come—it is the Lord who speaks—
I will pour out my spirit on all mankind.
Their sons and daughters shall prophesy,
your young men shall see visions,
your old men shall dream dreams.
¹⁸ Even on my slaves, men and women,
in those days, I will pour out my spirit.
¹⁹ I will display portents in heaven above
and signs on earth below.
²⁰ The sun will be turned into darkness
and the moon into blood
before the great Day of the Lord dawns.
²¹ All who call on the name of the Lord will be
saved.

²² "Men of Israel, listen to what I am going to say: Jesus the Nazarene was a man commended to you by God by the miracles and portents and signs that God worked through him when he was among you, as you all know. ·This man, who was put into your power by the deliberate intention and foreknowledge of God, you took and had crucified by men outside the Law. You killed him, but God raised him to life, freeing him from the pangs of Hades; for it was impossible for him to be held in its power since, ·as David says of him:

I saw the Lord before me always,
for with him at my right hand nothing can
shake me.

26   So my heart was glad
and my tongue cried out with joy;
my body, too, will rest in the hope

27   that you will not abandon my soul to Hades
nor allow your holy one to experience corruption.

28   You have made known the way of life to me,
you will fill me with gladness through your
presence.

29   "Brothers, no one can deny that the patriarch
David himself is dead and buried: his tomb is still
30   with us. ·But since he was a prophet, and knew
that God had sworn him an oath to make one of
31   his descendants succeed him on the throne, ·what
he foresaw and spoke about was the resurrection
of the Christ: he is the one who was not abandoned to Hades, and whose body did not experi-
32   ence corruption. ·God raised this man Jesus to life,
33   and all of us are witnesses to that. ·Now raised to
the heights by God's right hand, he has received
from the Father the Holy Spirit, who was promised, and what you see and hear is the outpouring
34   of that Spirit. ·For David himself never went up to
heaven; and yet these words are his:

The Lord said to my Lord:
Sit at my right hand
35   until I make your enemies
a footstool for you.

36   "For this reason the whole House of Israel can
be certain that God has made this Jesus whom you
crucified both Lord and Christ."

37   Hearing this, they were cut to the heart and said
to Peter and the apostles, "What must we do,
38   brothers?" ·"You must repent," Peter answered,
"and every one of you must be baptized in the
name of Jesus Christ for the forgiveness of your
sins, and you will receive the gift of the Holy
39   Spirit. ·The promise that was made is for you and

your children, and for all those who are far away,
for all those whom the Lord our God will call to
40 himself." •He spoke to them for a long time using
many arguments, and he urged them, "Save your-
41 selves from this perverse generation." •They were
convinced by his arguments, and they accepted
what he said and were baptized. That very day
about three thousand were added to their number.

☩

Most of us like to read or hear stories. They capture
our imagination and entertain us. But speeches are another matter. Most often they are long and boring and
give us a free pass to daydream. Yet there are some
speeches, such as Lincoln's Gettysburg Address and
Martin Luther King, Jr.'s, "I Have a Dream" speech,
which can turn our minds and hearts inside out.

These initial reflections on stories and speeches are
meant to get us into the spirit of appreciating Luke's
literary and theological style in Acts. Besides stories,
Acts has some twenty-eight speeches—e.g., the missionary speeches of Peter and Paul (see 2:14–41;
3:12–26; 13:16–41, etc.). All told, the speeches in
Acts account for about thirty per cent of the text. The
reader might well ask, Why does Luke dedicate so
much space to speeches? The answer is largely to be
found in the way historians of Luke's time applied
themselves to their task. For the ancient historian, the
speech and the deed were two sides of the same coin.
Tailored for its occasion, the speech gave insight into
the meaning of a historical event. Luke differs from
other ancient historians in that he uses speeches not
only to interpret the meaning of events but also to announce God's will. Luke is more concerned to preach
to his readers through the speeches of Acts than to
achieve tape-recorder accuracy of what was actually

said on a particular occasion. These observations may appear purely academic until we recall how the Gettysburg Address and Dr. King's "I Have a Dream" speech creatively interpreted the event of the abolition of slavery and "preached" its meaning. Or, nearer to our everyday experience, we recall the speech given at a silver-wedding-anniversary celebration. That speech recounted and interpreted twenty-five years of love exchanged and deepened. And in recounting and interpreting those twenty-five years, the speech inspired renewed dedication in the married couple and quickened fidelity in all who heard it.

Another illustration will help us appreciate a further aspect of Luke's use of speeches. If we were to read the collected speeches of a great speaker like Bishop Fulton Sheen, I venture that we would find a common pattern running through them—something which could be called the hallmark or signature of that person. Remember what we often say about an individual: "He's *always* talking about . . ." In most of Luke's speeches, especially in the missionary speeches of Peter and Paul, he follows a common pattern. That unmistakable pattern contains the following components: First, God has directed all the events of salvation; nothing has been left to chance. Second, the prophets foretold this salvation in the promises they made. Third, these promises have been fulfilled in Jesus, especially through God's resurrection of him. Fourth, the twelve apostles and Paul are witnesses to God's fulfillment of promises and proclaim this good news to all people. Fifth, repentance and conversion are demanded of those who hear the good news. In the comments on the speech of 2:14–41 and on the other speeches in Acts, we will have occasion to return to these five components which constitute the Lukan signature.

Luke is a consummate artist as he masterfully relates

speech to speech. Through careful planting, arrangement, and trimming of the shrubs of the speeches he has beautifully landscaped the property of Acts. For example, Peter's speech in Acts 2:14–41 is balanced in content by Paul's speech in Acts 13:16–41. By means of this captivating balance, Luke is telling his readers that Paul, a nonapostle, preaches the very same message as the chief of the apostles, Peter. Another example of Luke's artistry is found in the fact that a theme which is only one of the components (number one) in most of the speeches—namely, God's will controls salvation history—is the centerpiece of Paul's preaching in Acts 20:26–27. In that speech to the Ephesian elders Paul says: "And so here and now I swear that my conscience is clear as far as all of you are concerned, for I have without faltering put before you *the whole of God's purpose.*"

In summary, Luke uses the literary technique of his time, namely, the speeches of his chief characters, to interpret key events in his story and to preach to his community. We will now take a close look at Luke's craftsmanship in the speech of 2:14–41.

Through Peter's sermon in 2:14–41 Luke invites his readers to reflect upon the significance and implications of their contemporary experience of the Spirit. He does this by his techniques of linking speech to event and of having a five-component speech pattern. The Spirit-inspired preaching of the marvels of God (2:11) is the result of God's fulfillment of the prophecy of Joel. This theme of fulfillment of promise is not only the second component of Luke's pattern, but is also his way of expertly tailoring the speech to the deed of Pentecost (see 2:14–21). But this fulfillment of the Old Testament promise is possible only because God has fulfilled another, more important promise by not allowing David's descendant, Jesus, to see corruption: "Now raised to

the heights by God's right hand, he has received from
the Father the Holy Spirit, who was promised, and
what you see and hear is the outpouring of that Spirit"
(2:33; component three). And behind these two
fulfillments of promise stands God who controls all
things by his "deliberate intention and foreknowledge"
(2:33; component one). But no one would know anything whatsoever about God's fulfillment of his promises if the apostles were not witnesses to these events:
"God raised this man Jesus to life, and all of us are
witnesses to that" (2:32; component four). And this
fulfillment of promise is for all people (Luke's readers
and the Jews and gentiles to whom they preach on mission): "The promise that was made is for you and your
children, and for all those who are far away, for all
those whom the Lord our God will call to himself"
(2:39). This message of Peter and the Eleven (2:14)
calls for repentance (component five) because it is a
fulfillment of God's promises and thus is a manifestation of God. To be present before such a manifestation of God's will compels people to confess their
own sinfulness and to repent. But the greater motive
for the repentance of the Jewish listeners is the fact that
the Jews have rejected Jesus, God's fulfillment of promises (2:22). The promised Holy Spirit, experienced at
Pentecost, will come to those who believe in Jesus
crucified as Lord and Messiah (2:36) and who repent
of their sins (2:37–38).

"About three thousand were added to their number"
(2:41). Luke is no keeper of baptismal records. He
uses round numbers here to show that the thousands of
Jews who believe form the basis of repentant Israel.
The Christian community in Jerusalem stands in continuity with the Israel of the promises. It is heir of
God's promises, which have been fulfilled in Jesus and

which can be experienced today through the gift of the Spirit.

STUDY QUESTIONS: To what extent does the reception of Jesus' Spirit save us "from this perverse generation" (2:40)? Does Luke distort the event of Pentecost by composing Peter's speech to interpret that event? Is Luke correct in affirming that reception of the Spirit flows from belief that Jesus is Lord and consequently has the power to give such a divine gift?

Acts 2:42–47
THE EXPERIENCE OF SALVATION

42   These remained faithful to the teaching of the apostles, to the brotherhood, to the breaking of bread and to the prayers.

43   The many miracles and signs worked through the apostles made a deep impression on everyone.

44   The faithful all lived together and owned every-
45 thing in common; ·they sold their goods and possessions and shared out the proceeds among themselves according to what each one needed.

46   They went as a body to the Temple every day but met in their houses for the breaking of bread;
47 they shared their food gladly and generously; ·they praised God and were looked up to by everyone. Day by day the Lord added to their community those destined to be saved.

✠

This passage expresses in a nutshell what the first converts experienced because of the gift of the Holy Spirit. *"Save* yourselves from this perverse generation . . . about three thousand were *added* to their number" (2:40–41) and "Day by day the Lord *added* to their community those destined to be *saved"* (2:47b) bracket 2:42–47a. By means of this bracketing Luke highlights the elements itemized in 2:42–47a: Salvation in the community consists of these elements. Put another way, salvation is not pie in the sky, but is all these things experienced within the community, which faithfully continues the life and ministry of Jesus, who prayed, broke bread, taught in the Temple, enjoined the necessity of almsgiving and warned about the dangers of wealth, and was one in mind and heart with his male and female disciples.

This passage is also an advance summary of much of what will be narrated subsequently in Acts 3:1 to 5:42. In 3:1 to 4:22 Luke will narrate a sign and the consequences this healing has for the community's life. This sign examples 2:43: "The many miracles and signs worked through the apostles . . ." In 4:23–31 Luke will give a detailed example of "the prayers" mentioned in 2:42. In 4:36 to 5:11 he will provide a positive and a negative example of how to share material goods within the community (see 2:44–45). Acts 3:11–26, 4:8–12, and 5:29–32 will give representative samples of "the teaching of the apostles" (2:42).

This summary is not unique but is closely paralleled by the summaries of 4:32–35 and 5:12–16, as the following passages will demonstrate:

The many miracles and signs worked through the apostles made a deep impression on everyone. [Ac 2:43]

The apostles continued to testify to the resurrection of the Lord Jesus with great power, and they were all given great respect. [Ac 4:33]

So many signs and wonders were worked among the people at the hands of the apostles . . . [Ac 5:12a]

Other parallels between the three summary passages could be drawn—e.g., between 2:44–45 and 4:34–35 on the sharing of goods in common—but let this one parellel suffice to indicate the repetitive nature of these summaries. Luke seems to have composed these summaries, and did so by generalizing from particular occurrences like the healing of the cripple in 3:1–10. From that one miracle Luke generalized as the passages (2:43; 4:33; 5:12a) quoted above show.

Granted that we have detected Luke at work in the composition of these summaries, we can legitimately ask: Why are these three summaries so similar to one another? It seems that the threefold repetition of the same basic information in the summaries is Luke's way of underlining with heavy strokes the fact that Christian salvation will have these elements whenever and wherever it is experienced. Since Luke makes this point so forcefully early in his writing, he does not need to take time out to repeat it every time he describes how the Christian message came to a new town or was received by a new group of people. At times the mere mention of one element will suffice—for example, the occurrence of signs/miracles is mentioned at the beginning of the Christian mission in Samaria (see Ac 8:6, 13), the "breaking of bread" (Eucharist) is celebrated for the converts of Troas (see Ac 20:7, 11), and Paul, the founder of many Christian communities, shared his goods (see Ac 20:33–35).

STUDY QUESTIONS: Does our contemporary experience of Christian life and salvation encompass many of the elements detailed in the summary passage commented on here? Is it necessary for all Christians to experience every element comprised in salvation?

Acts 3:1–10
THE SPIRIT-FILLED APOSTLES
CONTINUE JESUS' MISSION

3 ¹ Once, when Peter and John were going up to the Temple for the prayers at the ninth hour, ² it happened that there was a man being carried past. He was a cripple from birth; and they used to put him down every day near the Temple entrance called the Beautiful Gate so that he could ³ beg from the people going in. ·When this man saw Peter and John on their way into the Temple he ⁴ begged from them. ·Both Peter and John looked ⁵ straight at him and said, "Look at us." ·He turned to them expectantly, hoping to get something ⁶ from them, ·but Peter said, "I have neither silver nor gold, but I will give you what I have: in the ⁷ name of Jesus Christ the Nazarene, walk!" ·Peter then took him by the hand and helped him to stand up. Instantly his feet and ankles became ⁸ firm, ·he jumped up, stood, and began to walk, and he went with them into the Temple, walking ⁹ and jumping and praising God. ·Everyone could ¹⁰ see him walking and praising God, ·and they recognized him as the man who used to sit begging at the Beautiful Gate of the Temple. They were all astonished and unable to explain what had happened to him.

✠

Our frequent reading of the Gospels may have dulled us to the significance of miracles. When we encounter this, the first miracle story of Acts, we might be tempted to remark unenthusiastically: "Oh, another miracle. How nice!" Perhaps some brainstorming may stir us to appreciation of this profoundly important miracle. Why do the apostles Peter and John perform this miracle in the Temple? What's in the name of Jesus Christ the Nazarene? How does this story relate to what follows?

In answering the why of the Temple, we should note that the Temple was the place where God's name or presence dwelt (see 1 K 8:27–30). In his final teaching —in the Temple—Jesus was graciously received by the people, but was schemed against by the religious leaders (see Lk 19:47–48). The Gospel of Luke ends with the observation, "and they were continually in the Temple praising God" (24:53). The first summary of Acts described the first believers as going in "a body to the Temple every day" (Ac 2:46). In the Temple the apostles continue Jesus' mission of teaching (see Ac 4: 2, 18). Acts 4:2, 17, 21; 5:13, 20, and 26 show the people of God as warmly receiving the apostles and their teaching in the Temple, whereas Acts 4:1, 5–6; 5:17, 18, and 21 depict the religious leaders as hostile to the apostles. In brief, in the Temple the apostles continue Jesus' mission of teaching and show how Christianity stands in continuity with Judaism.

Why the miracle? Peter's Pentecost speech used the prophecy of Joel to explain the past event of the gift of the Spirit and to give previews of the church's life, which would be characterized by "signs" and "the name" (Ac 2:14–21). Let us explore how this passage is the full-fledged version of the previews given in 2:14–21. First, the miracle of 3:1–10 is one of the "*signs* on earth below" which Luke portrays Joel as prophesying (see 2:19). By performing this sign, the Spirit-filled apostles, in the persons of Peter and John, follow in the footsteps of the Spirit-filled Jesus, whose mission was for the restoration of humankind (see the programmatic passages Luke 4:18–21 and 7:22, and the description of the Spirit-filled Jesus' mission in Acts 10:38). Empowered by Jesus' Spirit, the apostles restore a lame man to wholeness and in doing so fulfill what Isaiah prophesied would happen in the days of salvation: "then *the lame shall* leap like a deer" (Is 35:6; see Ac 3:8). In sum, the twelve apostles (and Paul; see Ac 14:8–10, where Paul performs a miracle very similar to that of 3:1–10) continue Jesus' work of doing good.

Second, the miracle of 3:1–10 gives full scope to another facet of the prophecy of Joel: "All who call on the *name* of the Lord will be saved" (Ac 2:21). It is in the power of this name, and not in the power of money, that Peter cures the cripple (3:6). We can get a grasp on the meaning of "name" if we note that in ancient thought the proper name of a person expressed that person's essence. By uttering that person's name, one made that person's power present. We glimpse some of the power of "the name" when we recall some of our common expressions: "It's not what you know, but who you know" or "Just mention my name, and they'll give you red-carpet treatment."

Consideration of the meaning of "name" leads us into the answer to the final question raised earlier by our brainstorming: How is 3:1–10 related to what follows? In what follows, the implications of Jesus' name (3:6) are spelled out (note the occurrences of "name" in 3:16; 4:7, 10–12, 17, 18, 30; 5:28, 40, 41). The miracle story of 3:1–10 causes ripples in the story of Acts which finally subside in 4:31 (see 4:22, where the age of the cripple is first mentioned; see further the conclusion of the prayer of 4:23–31: "by stretching out your hand *to heal or to work miracles and marvels through the name* of your servant Jesus" [4:30]). Put still another way, the signal event of 3:1–10 is inter-

preted by the speeches of Peter and the community's
prayer which occur in 3:11 to 4:31.

STUDY QUESTIONS: How does today's Christian church
continue the mission of the Spirit-
filled Jesus? Why is Jesus' name so
powerful?

GOD IS RESTORING HIS PEOPLE NOW

11 Everyone came running toward them in great excitement, to the Portico of Solomon, as it is called, where the man was still clinging to Peter 12 and John. ·When Peter saw the people he addressed them, "Why are you so surprised at this? Why are you staring at us as though we had made 13 this man walk by our own power or holiness? ·You are Israelites, and it is the God of Abraham, Isaac and Jacob, the God of our ancestors, who has glorified his servant Jesus, the same Jesus you handed over and then disowned in the presence of 14 Pilate after Pilate had decided to release him. ·It was you who accused the Holy One, the Just One, you who demanded the reprieve of a murderer 15 while you killed the prince of life. God, however, raised him from the dead, and to that fact we are 16 the witnesses; ·and it is the name of Jesus which, through our faith in it, has brought back the strength of this man whom you see here and who is well known to you. It is faith in that name that has restored this man to health, as you can all see.

17 "Now I know, brothers, that neither you nor your leaders had any idea what you were really 18 doing; ·this was the way God carried out what he had foretold, when he said through all his prophets 19 that his Christ would suffer. ·Now you must repent and turn to God, so that your sins may be wiped 20 out, ·and so that the Lord may send the time of comfort. Then he will send you the Christ he has 21 predestined, that is Jesus, ·whom heaven must keep till the universal restoration comes which God proclaimed, speaking through his holy 22 prophets. ·Moses, for example, said: The Lord God will raise up a prophet like myself for you,

from among your own brothers; you must listen
23 to whatever he tells you. ·The man who does not
listen to that prophet is to be cut off from the
24 people. ·In fact, all the prophets that have ever
spoken, from Samuel onward, have predicted
these days.
25   "You are the heirs of the prophets, the heirs of
the covenant God made with our ancestors when
he told Abraham: in your offspring all the families
26 of the earth will be blessed. ·It was for you in the
first place that God raised up his servant and sent
him to bless you by turning every one of you from
your wicked ways."

✠

In our comments on 2:14–41 we noted that speech
and event go hand in hand for Luke. This speech interprets the miracle of 3:1–10 and contains the typical
components of a Lukan speech: (1) God has directed
all events (3:18, 20); (2) the prophets have foretold
these events (3:18); (3) God's promises have been
fulfilled in Jesus (3:22–24); (4) the apostles are
witnesses (3:18); (5) repentance is called for (3:19).
Along with these five elements there are two additional components in the speech. First, the motif of ignorance. Since his hearers were *ignorant* of what they
were doing to Jesus (3:17), Peter's preaching offers
them another chance to repent. But the most important
new component is found in 3:20–21, which might be
more literally translated as: "and so that the Lord may
send the time of comfort and send you the Christ he
has predestined, that is Jesus, whom heaven must keep
till the time of the universal restoration comes which
God proclaimed, speaking through his holy prophets."
The key words here are "the time of the universal restoration." This phrase refers to an event which was expected to occur at the end of time. We can glimpse the

power of this phrase when we recall that we can restore a house to its original condition or restore a person to health and when we recall what contemporary prophets of doom proclaim as signs of the end of time: wars, meteors, the rapture, etc. What is attention-arresting in 3:20–21 is that Jesus' resurrection and exaltation to God's right hand have inaugurated the events of the end of time. "The days to come" spoken of by Joel (Ac 2:17) do not lie totally in the dim future; they have arrived in Jesus, and more specifically have arrived in the curing of the cripple in Jesus' name. All the prophets "have predicted *these days*" (3:24). The universal restoration has begun in the curing of the cripple: "it is faith in that name that *has restored* this man to health" (3:16).

One can express all these points from a different perspective by saying that Luke views the healing of the cripple in Jesus' name as an indication that God has begun to restore all things to their original harmony *now;* what was expected to occur only at the end of time, occurs now through Jesus. Begun in the present, the restoration of all will be culminated when Jesus returns in his second coming. When a person acknowledges that God has begun the expected restoration of Israel (see Ac 1:6–7) through Jesus and through miracles effected in his name, then one is called upon to repent. All those who listen to and believe in the prophet Jesus will not be cut off from the people (3:23). Like the prophet Elijah, Jesus has been raised up to call his people to repentance (3:26). For without repentance there can be no restoration. See Ecclesiasticus 48:10: Elijah was "designated in the prophecies of doom to allay God's wrath before the fury breaks, *to turn* the hearts of fathers toward their children, and *to restore* the tribes of Jacob."

In brief, Peter's speech uses prior Christian designations of Jesus such as "servant" (3:13), "holy one" (3:14), "just one" (3:14), and "author of life" (3:15) to describe who he is. It also employs an end-of-the-world understanding of the Messiah who will restore all things to interpret the miracle of healing (3:20-21). This miracle is the result of the restoration begun in Jesus. By repenting of their sins, the people can become participants in this restoration, a restoration to original harmony symbolized by the cripple's restoration to wholeness and health.

STUDY QUESTION: The people of Israel longed to be restored to their land and liberated from foreign domination. The prophets warned them that such restoration was not automatic, but that they should repent of their sins. Does this passage teach us Christians who believe in the power of Jesus' name anything about the meaning of repentance?

Acts 4:1–22
JESUS PROTECTS HIS MISSIONARIES

1 4 While they were still talking to the people the priests came up to them, accompanied by the 2 captain of the Temple and the Sadducees. ·They were extremely annoyed at their teaching the people the doctrine of the resurrection from the dead 3 by proclaiming the resurrection of Jesus. ·They arrested them, but as it was already late, they held 4 them till the next day. ·But many of those who had listened to their message became believers, the total number of whom had now risen to something like five thousand.

5 The next day the rulers, elders and scribes had 6 a meeting in Jerusalem ·with Annas the high priest, Caiaphas, Jonathan, Alexander and all the mem- 7 bers of the high-priestly families. ·They made the prisoners stand in the middle and began to interrogate them, "By what power, and by whose name 8 have you men done this?" ·Then Peter, filled with the Holy Spirit, addressed them, "Rulers of the 9 people, and elders! ·If you are questioning us today about an act of kindness to a cripple, and ask- 10 ing us how he was healed, ·then I am glad to tell you all, and would indeed be glad to tell the whole people of Israel, that it was by the name of Jesus Christ the Nazarene, the one you crucified, whom God raised from the dead, by this name and by no other that this man is able to stand up perfectly 11 healthy, here in your presence, today. ·This is the stone rejected by you the builders, but which has 12 proved to be the keystone. ·For of all the names in the world given to men, this is the only one by which we can be saved."

13 They were astonished at the assurance shown by Peter and John, considering they were unedu-

cated laymen; and they recognized them as asso-
14 ciates of Jesus; ·but when they saw the man who
had been cured standing by their side, they could
15 find no answer. ·So they ordered them to stand
outside while the Sanhedrin had a private discus-
16 sion. ·"What are we going to do with these men?"
they asked. "It is obvious to everybody in Jerusalem that a miracle has been worked through
17 them in public, and we cannot deny it. ·But to
stop the whole thing spreading any further among
the people, let us caution them never to speak to
anyone in this name again."
18   So they called them in and gave them a warning
on no account to make statements or to teach in
19 the name of Jesus. ·But Peter and John retorted,
"You must judge whether in God's eyes it is right
20 to listen to you and not to God. ·We cannot promise to stop proclaiming what we have seen and
21 heard." ·The court repeated the warnings and then
released them; they could not think of any way to
punish them, since all the people were giving glory
22 to God for what had happened. ·The man who had
been miraculously cured was over forty years old.

✠

Not long ago I spent nine days in Israel. I had so
much to see in so little time that often it was only in the
bus after visiting a famous site or at night over supper
that I learned that I had not seen some things which
others had. At times I felt an urge to return to a partic-
ularly impressive site the next "day at leisure." This
passage is like a famous site. It is dotted with so many
treasures that a brief tour of it may only scratch the
surface of its meaning. Readers should feel free to return to the passage at their leisure.

This passage is a further explication of the meaning
of the miracle of 3:1–10. Jesus' name and person are
for the salvation of the whole human being and not just
for that person's restoration to physical integrity. "For

of all the names in the world given to men, this is the only one by which we can be saved" (4:12). Acts 4:10–12 reflects the prophecy of Joel as it fulfills it: "All who call on the name of the Lord [i.e., "Jesus Christ the Nazarene, the one you crucified, whom God raised from the dead"] will be saved" (2:21).

Luke adroitly utilizes 4:1–4 to teach and to give a preview of coming attractions in Acts. In exercising his teaching prowess, Luke has no desire to chronicle history and thus does not shy away from narrating something in 4:1–4 which does not accord with historical fact. Historically, the Sadducees did not have authority to arrest anyone. Furthermore, if they considered teaching the resurrection to be a crime punishable by imprisonment, they would have had to lock up every Pharisee in the land. Luke uses 4:1–4 to teach that the people of Israel will follow the teaching of the apostles (see 4:1, 2, 4, 17, 21) whereas the Sadducees will oppose that teaching (see 4:1, 5–6). Note especially the contrast between 4:3 and 4:4: the leaders arrest the apostles, while the people believe the apostles' message. The rumblings of opposition surfacing in this passage preview 8:1: "that day a bitter persecution started against the church in Jerusalem. . . ." Moreover, Luke previews Paul's defense before the Sanhedrin, which is composed of Sadducees and Pharisees (see Ac 23:6–8 and 26:6–8). Paul is on trial for teaching the resurrection, which in Luke's view is the hallmark of Jewish faith and is Christianity's link with Judaism. While the numerous and influential Pharisees maintain belief in the resurrection, the Sadducees do not (23:8).

Luke also employs this story to present a word of comfort for the missionaries of his day who are subject to harassment and police surveillance: Jesus is faithful to the promise he made to protect those who preach in his name. Observe how Acts 4:8 is the fulfillment of

Jesus' promise in Luke 12:11–12 and how Acts 4:14 fulfills Luke 21:14–15:

> When they take you before synagogues and magistrates and authorities, do not worry about how to defend yourselves or what to say, because when the time comes, *the Holy Spirit* will teach you what you must say. [Lk 12:11–12]

> Then Peter, filled with *the Holy Spirit,* addressed them. [Ac 4:8; see also 4:13]

> Keep this carefully in mind: you are not to prepare your defense, because I myself shall give you an eloquence and a wisdom that none of your opponents will be able to resist or *contradict.* [Lk 21:14–15]

> They had nothing to say in *contradiction.* [Ac 4:14; a more literal translation than the JB's "they could find no answer"]

In summary, when the apostles teach the people "the doctrine of the resurrection from the dead by proclaiming the resurrection of Jesus" (4:2), they hand on the prized baton of Jewish tradition and show that Christianity is an authentic growth within Judaism. The opposition this message encounters should not discourage Luke's contemporary missionaries, for the Lord Jesus will protect them.

STUDY QUESTIONS: To what extent has today's Jewish-Christian dialogue alerted you to the beliefs which Jews and Christians have in common? Why is Luke concerned to point out the ways in which Christianity stands in continuity with Judaism?

23 As soon as they were released they went to the community and told them everything the chief
24 priests and elders had said to them. ·When they heard it they lifted up their voice to God all together. "Master," they prayed, "it is you who made heaven and earth and sea, and everything in
25 them; ·you it is who said through the Holy Spirit and speaking through our ancestor David, your servant:

Why this arrogance among the nations,
these futile plots among the peoples?
26 Kings on earth setting out to war,
princes making an alliance,
against the Lord and against his Anointed.

27 "This is what has come true: in this very city Herod and Pontius Pilate made an alliance with the pagan nations and the peoples of Israel, against your holy servant Jesus whom you
28 anointed, ·but only to bring about the very thing that you in your strength and your wisdom had
29 predetermined should happen. ·And now, Lord, take note of their threats and help your servants
30 to proclaim your message with all boldness, ·by stretching out your hand to heal and to work miracles and marvels through the name of your holy
31 servant Jesus." ·As they prayed, the house where they were assembled rocked; they were all filled with the Holy Spirit and began to proclaim the word of God boldly.

✠

This section is the climax of the story begun in

3:1–10 and focuses the reader's attention on some of Luke's major themes: mission, persecution, and prayer.

Mission. In response to its prayer the community receives the gift of the Holy Spirit, who empowers it to embark on bold missionary proclamation of the word/message (see the commentary on 2:1–13 and Ac 4:29, 31; 8:25; 11:19–20; 13:46; 14:25; 16:6, 32).

Persecution. When the community's missionaries encounter opposition, the community finds support in prayer (see also Ac 12:5: "All the time Peter was under guard the Church prayed to God for him unremittingly"). In its prayer the Christian community reflects on what God has done for his people in the past. Thus the prayer in 4:24 is modeled on the prayer uttered by King Hezekiah when Judah was harassed by Sennacherib (see Is 37:16–20). The community also looks back on the way God acted for the persecuted Jesus and draws inspiration from Jesus' example. The words in 4:27 show how the community viewed what happened to Jesus during his trial before Pilate and Herod as a fulfillment of Psalm 2:1–2 (as quoted in Acts 4:25–26). Behind Sennacherib's attack on Judah, behind Jesus' trial, and behind the persecution of the community stands God's will: "But only to bring about the very thing that you in your strength and wisdom had predetermined should happen" (4:28). The powers that be may rage and storm, but they cannot thwart God's will. The Christian community is confident that its God will triumph even though his enemies seem victorious as in the case of Jesus.

Prayer. By its life of prayer and communion with God (see Ac 2:42–47) the community follows in the footsteps of Jesus and is in contact with God's will and power through the gift of the Holy Spirit. See Luke 11:13: God will "give *the Holy Spirit* to those who ask him," as contrasted with Matthew 7:11: God will "give *good things* to those who ask him." Luke uses a contemporary motif to demonstrate that the community's prayer has been heard—the shaking of the house (4:31). This motif is found for example in Virgil's *Aeneid:* "Scarcely had I thus spoken, when suddenly it seemed all things trembled, the doors and laurels of the god; the whole hill shook round about and the tripod moaned as the shrine was thrown open" (III, 90–92, Loeb translation).

STUDY QUESTIONS: Does this section provide any help on how to formulate our prayers? Does this section lend credibility to the ancient Christian maxim that persecution nurtures the growth of the church?

Acts 4:32 to 5:11
COMMUNITY UNITY FOSTERED OR THREATENED BY POSSESSIONS

32 The whole group of believers was united, heart and soul; no one claimed for his own use anything that he had, as everything they owned was held in common.

33 The apostles continued to testify to the resurrection of the Lord Jesus with great power, and they were all given great respect.

34 None of their members was ever in want, as all those who owned land or houses would sell them,

35 and bring the money from them, ·to present it to the apostles; it was then distributed to any members who might be in need.

36 There was a Levite of Cypriot origin called Joseph whom the apostles surnamed Barnabas

37 (which means "son of encouragement"). ·He owned a piece of land and he sold it and brought the money, and presented it to the apostles.

5 There was another man, however, called Ananias. He and his wife, Sapphira, agreed to

2 sell a property; ·but with his wife's connivance he kept back part of the proceeds, and brought the

3 rest and presented it to the apostles. ·"Ananias," Peter said, "how can Satan have so possessed you that you should lie to the Holy Spirit and keep

4 back part of the money from the land? ·While you still owned the land, wasn't it yours to keep, and after you had sold it wasn't the money yours to do with as you liked? What put this scheme into your mind? It is not to men that you have lied, but to

5 God." ·When he heard this Ananias fell down dead. This made a profound impression on every-

⁶ one present. ·The younger men got up, wrapped
the body in a sheet, carried it out and buried it.

⁷   About three hours later his wife came in, not
⁸ knowing what had taken place. ·Peter challenged
her, "Tell me, was this the price you sold the land
⁹ for?" "Yes," she said, "that was the price." ·Peter
then said, "So you and your husband have agreed
to put the Spirit of the Lord to the test! What
made you do it? You hear those footsteps? They
have just been to bury your husband; they will
¹⁰ carry you out, too." ·Instantly she dropped dead
at his feet. When the young men came in they
found she was dead, and they carried her out and
¹¹ buried her by the side of her husband. ·This made
a profound impression on the whole Church and
on all who heard it.

✠

Sharing of possessions bespeaks unity and community. A married couple share the same bed and board.
A friend says, "What's mine is yours." The spoiled brat
threatens the very existence of the neighborhood football game with, "If you don't play the game my way,
I'll take my football and go home." In some parts of
the United States people leave their doors unlocked
when they're out shopping; friends are expected to
walk right in and make themselves at home. A boy
friend knows that he's accepted into the family when he
can raid the icebox.

These contemporary examples of sharing of possessions will help us appreciate the meaning of this passage, which treats the meanings of unity and possessions in four vignettes: (1) 4:32 highlights friendship;
(2) 4:34–35 is the fulfillment of Deuteronomy
15:4–5; (3) 4:36–37 gives the sterling example of the
generous Barnabas; (4) 5:1–11 narrate the face-
blanching horror tale of Ananias and Sapphira.

Friendship. Acts 4:32 uses the Greco-Roman terminology of friendship to explain the unity which the primitive Christian community experienced as a result of the gift of the Holy Spirit (see 4:31 and also 2:44). In his *Nicomachean Ethics,* Aristotle observes: ". . . for it has been said already that all the feelings that constitute friendship for others are an extension of regard for self. Moreover, all the proverbs agree with this; for example, 'Friends have *one soul* between them,' *'Friends' goods are common property'* " (IX, 8, 2, Loeb translation, italics added). Cicero notes: "Nothing, moreover, is more conducive to love and intimacy than compatibility of character in good men; for when two people have the same ideals and the same tastes, it is a natural consequence that each loves the other as himself; and the result is, as Pythagoras requires of ideal friendship, that *several are united in one*" (*De officiis,* I, 17, 56, Loeb translation, italics added). The primitive Christian community holds all things in common and is united heart and soul. Their love for one another prompts them to share their goods. By using Greco-Roman terminology about friendship, Luke challenges his rich Greco-Roman Christian readers to be open to the unity which the Holy Spirit strives to effect among poor and rich members of the church, members whose economic status previously prevented them from becoming friends.

Fulfillment of Deuteronomy 15:4–5. "*None of their members was ever in want*" (4:34) fulfills Deuteronomy 15:4–5, especially in its Greek translation: "*Let there be no one in want among you then.* For Yahweh will bless you in the land Yahweh your God gives you for your inheritance only if you pay careful attention to the voice of Yahweh, your God, keeping and observing all these commandments that I enjoin on you today." Because the primitive Christian community, which inherits God's Old Testament promises, has observed Yahweh's laws of almsgiving and care for the needy, they have been blessed with unity in the land.

Barnabas, promoter of Christian unity. Acts 4:36–37 and 5:1–11 are positive and negative examples of how to promote Christian unity within the community. Barnabas, about whose missionary work Luke will have much more to say in later chapters, is a non-Jerusalemite. He "presents it [the money] to the apostles" (4:37). This phrase, which is more literally translated as "laid it at the feet of the apostles," also occurs in 4:35 and 5:2 and literarily unites this entire section. When we explore the symbolism of "laying something at the feet of someone else," we realize that there is also a theological unity within the entire section. Recall how Luke describes the return of the cured Samaritan leper: and he "threw himself *at the feet* of Jesus and thanked him" (Lk 17:16). The primitive Christians Barnabas and Ananias, by laying money at the feet of the apostles, show that they submit to the authority of the apostles, an authority which is chillingly depicted in 5:1–11.

Ananias and Sapphira. The message of this awful story is that the premeditated worship of mammon, acted out in the conduct of Ananias and Sapphira, disrupts the unity of the community; the Lord, through the apostles, punishes the disrupters with expulsion from the community. The use of the same rare Greek verb in Acts 5:2 and in the Greek translation of Joshua 7:1 suggests that Luke has used the story of Achan in Joshua 7 as a model for the story of Ananias and Sapphira. There are other similarities between the stories of Joshua 7 and Acts 5:1–11. Both Achan and Ananias/Sapphira try to decieve God by holding back goods. Both are confronted by God's spokesman: Joshua in the case of Achan, and Peter in the case of Ananias/Sapphira. Both are cast out of the community by death. Their attachment to possessions (in Joshua 7:21 Achan is said to have coveted the banned goods) disrupts community life.

The Lukan story of Judas also seems to have served as a model for the composition of this almost un-Christian story. "How can Satan have so possessed you" (5:3) recalls "then Satan entered into Judas" (Lk 22:3). Judas, who presumably had left all to follow Jesus (see Lk 18:28), "bought a field with the money he was paid for his crime" (Ac 1:18). Like Judas, Ananias and Sapphira are influenced by Satan and succumb to the temptation of money. Judas betrays Jesus for money, sets up homesteading with the money, and dies suddenly (see Ac 1:18 for the gruesome details). Ananias and Sapphira connive (5:2), keep back part of the proceeds from their sale of land, "put the Spirit of the Lord to the test" by trying to deceive the Spirit-filled Peter (5:9), and perish suddenly. In brief, Luke creates a tale in which the sudden demise of Ananias and Sapphira apprise his readers of the high stakes for which the game of Christian sharing is played.

STUDY QUESTIONS: Does this passage tell us that poverty was an ideal of the primitive Christian community? Some rich parishes share their money and lives with poorer parishes. Is this horizon-broadening scheme, or one like it, possible between rich and poor families, between rich and poor nations?

Acts 5:12–16
THE AUTHORITY OF THE APOSTLES

^{12b} They all used to meet by common consent in the
¹³ Portico of Solomon. ·No one else ever dared to
join them, but the people were loud in their praise
¹⁴ and the numbers of men and women who came to
^{12a} believe in the Lord increased steadily. ·So many
signs and wonders were worked among the people
¹⁵ at the hands of the apostles ·that the sick were
even taken out into the streets and laid on beds
and sleeping mats in the hope that at least the
shadow of Peter might fall across some of them
¹⁶ as he went past. ·People even came crowding in
from the towns around about Jerusalem, bringing
with them their sick and those tormented by unclean spirits, and all of them were cured.

☩

This is the third and final summary within chapters
2–5 (see the commentaries on 2:42–47 and 4:32–35).
In the smoother version of the passage, occasioned by
the JB's rearrangement of verse 12a, three points leap
out and beckon for attention: (1) the people praise the
apostles (5:13); (2) the number of believers increases
(5:14); (3) the authority of the apostles is graphically
illustrated (5:12a, 15–16). Since the commentary on
4:1–22 noted the significance of the praise of the people, we will not comment further on point one. The notion of the increase of believers has been sufficiently
commented on in 2:41 and 47 and 4:4. What needs
additional comment is point three, the authority of the
apostles.

Peter's shadow heals people. Small wonder that people flock to him from towns around about Jerusalem to be cured (5:16). Why this strange, almost magical notion about healing power after Luke has painstakingly demonstrated in chapters 3–4 that the cure of the cripple was done *in the name of Jesus?* "Why are you staring at us as though we had made this man walk by our own power or holiness?" (3:12). Why these two vastly different conceptions of miracle-working power? Perhaps an example of "contradictory" proverbs will hint at an answer: we say, "Out of sight, out of mind," as well as, "Distance lends enchantment." Which of these contradictory proverbs more adequately describes the experience of friends? Have you, perhaps, experienced the truth of each of the proverbs with the very same person? As Luke perceives the authority of the Spirit-filled apostles, he is convinced that their power comes from the Lord Jesus and uses much ink to underline that point in chapters 3–4. Luke also wanted to depict the power of the Spirit-filled apostles by means of an image which his non-Jewish contemporaries could readily understand. He selected the image of shadow. As a recent commentator, P. W. van der Horst, has shown, "to be touched by a man's shadow means to be in contact with his soul or his essence and to be influenced by that, whether it be for the better or for the worse" (*New Testament Studies* 23 [1976/77], 204–12). A good example of this mentality is found in the words the Roman dramatist Ennius puts into the mouth of Thyestes. Thyestes, with a crime weighing heavily on his conscience, pleads: "Strangers, draw you not near to me! Back there, back! Lest a tainted touch from me, *lest my very shadow harm you that are sound.* Oh, such a deadly violence of sin clings to my body" (in the Loeb translation of Cicero's *Tusculan Disputations;* italics added). What more graphic way could

Luke have found to tell his contemporary non-Jewish readers about the authority of the apostles? Not only are their words powerful, why their very shadow cures! (See what power is attributed to handkerchiefs touched to the body of Paul in Acts 19:11–12.) As in the case of the two proverbs we utilized above as illustrations, Luke's two views of miracles must be balanced one against the other to find the "truth."

STUDY QUESTION: Does it shock you that Luke made use of the image of a shadow—something we moderns would call magical—to describe the authority of the apostles?

THIS MOVEMENT COMES FROM GOD

17   Then the high priest intervened with all his supporters from the party of the Sadducees.
18 Prompted by jealousy, ·they arrested the apostles and had them put in the common jail.

19   But at night the angel of the Lord opened the
20 prison gates and said as he led them out, ·"Go and stand in the Temple, and tell the people all about
21 this new Life." ·They did as they were told; they went into the Temple at dawn and began to preach.

    When the high priest arrived, he and his supporters convened the Sanhedrin—this was the full Senate of Israel—and sent to the jail for them to be
22 brought. ·But when the officials arrived at the prison they found they were not inside, so they
23 went back and reported, ·"We found the jail securely locked and the warders on duty at the gates, but when we unlocked the door we found
24 no one inside." ·When the captain of the Temple and the chief priests heard this news they won-
25 dered what this could mean. ·Then a man arrived with fresh news. "At this very moment," he said, "the men you imprisoned are in the Temple. They
26 are standing there preaching to the people." ·The captain went with his men and fetched them. They were afraid to use force in case the people stoned them.

27   When they had brought them in to face the Sanhedrin, the high priest demanded an explanation.
28 "We gave you a formal warning," he said, "not to preach in this name, and what have you done? You have filled Jerusalem with your teaching, and seem determined to fix the guilt of this man's
29 death on us." ·In reply Peter and the apostles said,

"Obedience to God comes before obedience to ³⁰ men; ·it was the God of our ancestors who raised up Jesus, but it was you who had him executed by ³¹ hanging on a tree. ·By his own right hand God has now raised him up to be leader and savior, to give repentance and forgiveness of sins through him to ³² Israel. ·We are witnesses to all this, we and the Holy Spirit whom God has given to those who ³³ obey him." ·This so infuriated them that they wanted to put them to death.

³⁴   One member of the Sanhedrin, however, a Pharisee called Gamaliel, who was a doctor of the Law and respected by the whole people, stood up and asked to have the men taken outside for a ³⁵ time. ·Then he addressed the Sanhedrin, "Men of Israel, be careful how you deal with these people. ³⁶ There was Theudas who became notorious not so long ago. He claimed to be someone important, and he even collected about four hundred followers; but when he was killed, all his followers ³⁷ scattered and that was the end of them. ·And then there was Judas the Galilean, at the time of the census, who attracted crowds of supporters; but he got killed too, and all his followers dispersed. ³⁸ What I suggest, therefore, is that you leave these men alone and let them go. If this enterprise, this movement of theirs, is of human origin it will ³⁹ break up of its own accord; ·but if it does in fact come from God you will not only be unable to destroy them, but you might find yourselves fighting against God."

⁴⁰   His advice was accepted; ·and they had the apostles called in, gave orders for them to be flogged, warned them not to speak in the name of ⁴¹ Jesus and released them. ·And so they left the presence of the Sanhedrin glad to have had the honor of suffering humiliation for the sake of the name.

⁴²   They preached every day both in the Temple and in private houses, and their proclamation of the Good News of Christ Jesus was never interrupted.

✠

The perceptive reader may have raised some questions about this section. It seems to be a repetition of 4:1–22. The supernaturally engineered prison break of 5:19–21 doesn't even merit a passing comment in the trial scene of 5:27–33. Gamaliel's advice to "leave these men alone and let them go" (5:38) carries the day (5:39), but then the Sanhedrin acts in ignorance of it by ordering the apostles to be flogged (5:40). Vigorously healthy men have died from forty lashes less one. Can we discern Luke's message behind these puzzling features?

While this section has a number of features in common with the trial of 4:1–22, it adds significantly to the progress of the story of Acts. The authorities are "jealous" (5:18) of the apostles, to whom the people listen so eagerly that they would stone anyone who would dare to take the apostles away with force (5:26). The powerful Jewish authorities are humorously depicted as perplexed (5:24); not even their strong prison can detain the apostles from their appointed task of leading the people. The powerless apostles, not the Sanhedrin, are in control; they are the new leaders of God's people. Israel is to be found in the person of the apostles and in the people who obey their teaching (5:20–21, 26, 28), which fills Jerusalem, the city of God's promises (5:28).

The miraculous prison break of 5:19–21 is a literary motif (see also 12:6–11 and 16:26–27) which Luke shares with other religious historians of his day. In his book *Concerning the Jews* Artapanus, a first-century B.C. Jewish historian, rewrites part of the Moses story in this way: "And Moses took courage and determined to lead a hostile force against the Egyptians. . . . And when the king of the Egyptians had learned of Moses' coming, he summoned him before him and inquired why he had come. And he said because the Lord of the world had commanded him to set the Jews free. And when he learned this, the king confined him to prison. But when night came, *the doors of the prison opened of their own accord,* and some of guards died, while some were overcome with sleep and their weapons were broken. And Moses went out and came to the palace" (see D. L. Tiede, *The Charismatic Figure as Miracle Worker,* pp. 321–22; italics added). By means of this literary motif of a miraculous prison break Luke playfully celebrates God's protective power. Luke encourages the persecuted missionaries of his church that the progress of God's Word will not be hindered by the imprisonment of its preachers. But, as he will almost immediately show in the tragic story of Stephen (6:8 to 7:60), Luke also appreciates and takes most seriously fully orchestrated hostility to God's messengers. Sometimes blood will be shed before the Word triumphs. Luke flirts with the joyful aspect of the mystery of Christian suffering in 5:41: "And so they left the presence of the Sanhedrin *glad to have had the honor* of suffering humiliation for the sake of the name." This verse recalls Luke's fourth beatitude: "Happy are you when people hate you, drive you out, abuse you, denounce your name as criminal, on account of the Son of Man. Rejoice when that day comes and dance for joy, then your reward will be great in heaven" (Lk 6:22–23).

Gamaliel gives the advice which Luke wants his readers to hear and hear clearly: Don't persecute the Christians; if what they are about is not from God, it will self-destruct in due time. Through his delineation of Gamaliel Luke makes a further point about the religious authorities. They must obey God as he is preached by the apostles (5:29–32). And part of that obedience to God is repentance of what they have done to Jesus (5:28, 31). Yet they—Gamaliel included—take a wait-and-see attitude and do not obey and repent. How can they lead the people of God when they don't obey the God of the people? The apostles are the new leaders of God's people.

STUDY QUESTIONS: Can Luke's use of the miraculous-release-from-prison motif lead Christians to expect that God should free them from their problems in some similar fashion? Why would anyone be "glad to have had the honor of suffering humiliation for the sake of the name" (5:41)?

Acts 6:1–7
THE HELLENISTIC MISSIONARIES ARE SUBJECT TO THE APOSTLES

¹ 6 About this time, when the number of disciples was increasing, the Hellenists made a complaint against the Hebrews: in the daily distribu-
² tion their own widows were being overlooked. ·So the Twelve called a full meeting of the disciples and addressed them, "It would not be right for us to neglect the word of God so as to give out food;
³ you, brothers, must select from among yourselves seven men of good reputation, filled with the Spirit and with wisdom; we will hand over this
⁴ duty to them, ·and continue to devote ourselves
⁵ to prayer and to the service of the word." ·The whole assembly approved of this proposal and elected Stephen, a man full of faith and of the Holy Spirit, together with Philip, Prochorus, Nicanor, Timon, Parmenas, and Nicolaus of
⁶ Antioch, a convert to Judaism. ·They presented these to the apostles, who prayed and laid their hands on them.
⁷ The word of the Lord continued to spread: the number of disciples in Jerusalem was greatly increased, and a large group of priests made their submission to the faith.

✠

This section is a hinge passage which binds what has gone before to what is to follow. The hinge is twofold: (1) increase of believers; (2) authority of the apostles.

Verses one and seven repeat the refrain of increase of numbers which Luke sounded in 2:41, 4:4, and

5:14. An increase of believers is a sure sign that God is blessing the Christian movement (see 5:39). Acts 6:7 also states that "a large group of priests" joined the Christians. Conversion to Jesus Christ is not limited to one group within Judaism (see 15:5 on the conversion of some of the Pharisees). This motif of increase of numbers directs the reader's attention to chapters 6–8, in which Luke will show how Jesus' promise in Acts 1:8 is being fulfilled as the missionaries Stephen and Philip, respectively, challenge the diaspora Jews in Jerusalem and evangelize Samaria and an Ethiopian eunuch.

The authority of the Twelve (6:2, the only passage in Acts which speaks of the Twelve) is highlighted by the facts that they make the initial proposal for the creation of the Seven, give its rationale (6:2–5), and convey power by laying hands on the seven Hellenists (6:6). The apostles (6:6), who according to Luke have to abide in Jerusalem as the bond of continuity with Judaism (see 8:1), approve missionary expansion by Hellenists like Stephen and Philip (see 8:14–17).

There are a number of problems lurking behind the scenes of the theme of the authority of the apostles. It is not perfectly clear what the problem was between the Hellenists (Jews who spoke only Greek) and the Hebrews (Jews who could speak Greek, but also knew a Semitic tongue). If twelve men could not handle the daily distribution of food, how would the lesser number of seven do any better? While it is said that the Seven are charged with the daily dole, Luke nowhere narrates the fulfillment of this charge. Those Luke singles out from the Seven—Stephen and Philip—do what the apostles do: preach the Word and pray (see 6:2, 4). Luke seems to have taken over a tradition which championed the Seven as Spirit-filled, independent Hellenistic missionaries and to have incorporated that tradition into his story by making the Seven subservient to the apostles.

STUDY QUESTIONS: Does Luke's stress on the criterion of dedication to preaching the Word and prayer say anything about the responsibilities of Christian ministers today? Was everything in the primitive Christian community as tension-free as Acts 2:41-47 might seem to indicate?

Acts 6:8–15
STEPHEN, SOURCE OF ENCOURAGEMENT

8 Stephen was filled with grace and power and began to work miracles and great signs among the
9 people. ·But then certain people came forward to debate with Stephen, some from Cyrene and Alexandria who were members of the synagogue called the Synagogue of Freedmen, and others from
10 Cilicia and Asia. ·They found they could not get the better of him because of his wisdom, and because it was the Spirit that prompted what he said.
11 So they procured some men to say, "We heard him using blasphemous language against Moses and
12 against God." ·Having in this way turned the people against him as well as the elders and scribes, they took Stephen by surprise, and arrested him
13 and brought him before the Sanhedrin. ·There they put up false witnesses to say, "This man is always making speeches against this Holy Place and the
14 Law. ·We have heard him say that Jesus the Nazarene is going to destroy this Place and alter the
15 traditions that Moses handed down to us." ·The members of the Sanhedrin all looked intently at Stephen, and his face appeared to them like the face of an angel.

✠

With this section Luke swings his camera away from the apostles and begins to focus it on two of the Seven (see 6:1–7). Acts 6:8 to 8:3 is dedicated to Stephen; Acts 8:4–40 deals with Philip.

This section also introduces the culmination of the trial scenes in the Jerusalem phase of Acts. In 4:1–22

Peter and John are warned and released. In 5:17–42 the apostles are flogged and released. In 6:8 to 8:3 Stephen is stoned and buried. The reader should note that similar trial scenes occupy much of the last part of Acts: 23:1–11 (Paul before the Sanhedrin); 24:10–21 (Paul before Felix); 26:1–32 (Paul before King Agrippa). In each of these six trial scenes Luke's primary concern is not the defense of the apostles, Stephen, or Paul. Rather his concern is to show how Jesus and Christianity are related to Judaism and God's promises.

Under attack from unfriendly folk, Stephen is graced with irresistible wisdom and the power of the Spirit (6:10). Jesus' promises are fulfilled. "I myself shall give you an eloquence and a wisdom that none of your opponents will be able to resist or contradict" (Lk 21:15). When the time of persecution occurs, "the Holy Spirit will teach you what you must say" (Lk 12:12). That Jesus does fulfill his promises of help is a great source of encouragement to missionaries in Luke's community who find themselves in situations similar to that of Stephen. Stephen's angelic countenance symbolizes that God is for Stephen (6:15).

Accusations by false witnesses that Jesus said that he would destroy the Temple (6:13–14) recall Mark's account of Jesus' trial: "Some stood up and submitted this false evidence against him, 'We heard him say, "I am going to destroy this Temple made by human hands, and in three days build another, not made by human hands"'" (Mk 14:57–58). In his own account of Jesus' trial Luke has omitted the details of false witnesses and Jesus' claim to destroy the Temple for insertion here. In this respect as in others (see commentary on Ac 7:54 to 8:3) Stephen's trial and death recall Jesus'. Out of the rubble of trial, persecution, and death God will raise up missionaries to spread the Word (see 8:1–4 and 11:19).

STUDY QUESTION: In this section Stephen seems to do everything but attend to the daily distribution of food (see 6:1–2). Why does Luke portray Stephen as a great miracle-worker and preacher?

Acts 7:1–53
THE PRESENT ILLUMINES THE PAST

$\frac{1}{2}$ 7 The high priest asked, "Is this true?" ·He replied, "My brothers, my fathers, listen to what I have to say. The God of glory appeared to our ancestor Abraham, while he was in Mesopotamia
3 before settling in Haran, ·and said to him, 'Leave your country and your family and go to the land
4 I will show you.' ·So he left Chaldaea and settled in Haran; and after his father died God made him leave Haran and come to this land where you are
5 living today. ·God did not give him a single square foot of this land to call his own, yet he promised to give it to him and after him to his descendants,
6 childless though he was. ·The actual words God used when he spoke to him are that his descendants would be exiles in a foreign land, where they would be slaves and oppressed for four hundred
7 years. ·'But I will pass judgment on the nation that enslaves them,' God said, 'and after this they will
8 leave and worship me in this place.' ·Then he made the covenant of circumcision: so when his son Isaac was born he circumcised him on the eighth day. Isaac did the same for Jacob, and Jacob for the twelve patriarchs.
9 "The patriarchs were jealous of Joseph and sold him into slavery in Egypt. But God was with him,
10 and rescued him from all his miseries by making him wise enough to attract the attention of Pharaoh king of Egypt, who made him governor of Egypt and put him in charge of the royal house-
11 hold. ·Then a famine came that caused much suffering throughout Egypt and Canaan, and our an-
12 cestors could find nothing to eat. ·When Jacob heard that there was grain for sale in Egypt, he
13 sent our ancestors there on a first visit, ·but it was

on the second that Joseph made himself known to
his brothers, and told Pharaoh about his family.
14 Joseph then sent for his father Jacob and his whole
15 family, a total of seventy-five people. ·Jacob went
down into Egypt and after he and our ancestors
16 had died there, ·their bodies were brought back to
Shechem and buried in the tomb that Abraham
had bought and paid for from the sons of Hamor,
the father of Shechem.

17 "As the time drew near for God to fulfill the
promise he had solemnly made to Abraham, our
18 nation in Egypt grew larger and larger, ·until a
new king came to power in Egypt who knew
19 nothing of Joseph. ·He exploited our race, and ill-
treated our ancestors, forcing them to expose their
20 babies to prevent their surviving. ·It was at this
period that Moses was born, a fine child and fa-
vored by God. He was looked after for three
21 months in his father's house, ·and after he had
been exposed, Pharaoh's daughter adopted him
22 and brought him up as her own son. ·So Moses was
taught all the wisdom of the Egyptians and became a man with power both in his speech and his
actions.

23 "At the age of forty he decided to visit his coun-
24 trymen, the sons of Israel. ·When he saw one of
them being ill-treated he went to his defense and
25 rescued the man by killing the Egyptian. ·He
thought his brothers realized that through him
26 God would liberate them, but they did not. ·The
next day, when he came across some of them
fighting, he tried to reconcile them. 'Friends,' he
said, 'you are brothers; why are you hurting each
27 other?' ·But the man who was attacking his fellow
countryman pushed him aside. 'And who appointed you,' he said, 'to be our leader and judge?
28 Do you intend to kill me as you killed the Egyp-
29 tian yesterday?' ·Moses fled when he heard this
and he went to stay in the land of Midian, where
he became the father of two sons.

30 "Forty years later, in the wilderness near Mount
Sinai, an angel appeared to him in the flames of a

³¹ bush that was on fire. ·Moses was amazed by what
he saw. As he went nearer to look at it the voice
³² of the Lord was heard, ·'I am the God of your an-
cestors, the God of Abraham, Isaac and Jacob.'
Moses trembled and did not dare to look any
³³ more. ·The Lord said to him, 'Take off your shoes;
the place where you are standing is holy ground.
³⁴ I have seen the way my people are ill-treated in
Egypt, I have heard their groans, and I have come
down to liberate them. So come here and let me
send you into Egypt.'

³⁵   "It was the same Moses that they had disowned
when they said, 'Who appointed you to be our
leader and judge?' who was now sent to be both
leader and redeemer through the angel who had
³⁶ appeared to him in the bush. ·It was Moses who,
after performing miracles and signs in Egypt, led
them out across the Red Sea and through the wil-
³⁷ derness for forty years. ·It was Moses who told
the sons of Israel, 'God will raise up a prophet like
myself for you from among your own brothers.'
³⁸ When they held the assembly in the wilderness it
was only through Moses that our ancestors could
communicate with the angel who had spoken to
him on Mount Sinai; it was he who was entrusted
³⁹ with words of life to hand on to us. ·This is the
man that our ancestors refused to listen to: they
pushed him aside, turned back to Egypt in their
⁴⁰ thoughts, ·and said to Aaron, 'Make some gods to
be our leaders; we do not understand what has
come over this Moses who led us out of Egypt.'
⁴¹ It was then that they made a bull calf and offered
sacrifice to the idol. They were perfectly happy
with something they had made for themselves.
⁴² God turned away from them and abandoned them
to the worship of the army of heaven, as scripture
says in the book of the prophets:

> Did you bring me victims and sacrifices in the
> wilderness
> for all those forty years, you House of Israel?

43   No, you carried the tent of Moloch on your
           shoulders
       and the star of the god Rephan,
       those idols that you had made to adore.
       So now I will exile you even further than
           Babylon.

44   "While they were in the desert our ancestors
       possessed the Tent of Testimony that had been
       constructed according to the instructions God
       gave Moses, telling him to make an exact copy of
45   the pattern he had been shown. ·It was handed
       down from one ancestor of ours to another until
       Joshua brought it into the country we had con-
       quered from the nations which were driven out by
       God as we advanced. Here it stayed until the time
46   of David. ·He won God's favor and asked permis-
       sion to have a temple built for the House of Jacob,
47   though it was Solomon who actually built God's
48   house for him. ·Even so the Most High does not
       live in a house that human hands have built: for
       as the prophet says:

49   With heaven my throne
       and earth my footstool,
       what house could you build me,
       what place could you make for my rest?
50   Was not all this made by hand?

51   "You stubborn people, with your pagan hearts
       and pagan ears. You are always resisting the Holy
52   Spirit, just as your ancestors used to do. ·Can you
       name a single prophet your ancestors never per-
       secuted? In the past they killed those who foretold
       the coming of the Just One, and now you have
53   become his betrayers, his murderers. ·You who
       had the Law brought to you by angels are the very
       ones who have not kept it."

✠

If I might rephrase an old radio slogan, don't turn
that page. Don't turn your back on this long, long, long

speech of Stephen. Be patient. I can assure you that you haven't been paired with the bore of the month. The raising of three pertinent questions will make Stephen's speech sparkle and glisten with meaning.

Over the years commentators have puzzled over the question of why Stephen's speech doesn't fit its context. Stephen is accused of blasphemy against Moses and God, and of making speeches against the Temple and the Law (6:11–14). Yet in his long, meandering speech Stephen does not address himself to these charges. This incongruity could be compared to a person accused of the most heinous crimes defending himself by narrating the history of his country. *Why the incongruity?* It seems that there is only an incongruity when the reader assumes that Luke is concerned to narrate chroniclelike history and to recount how Stephen answered his accusers. Luke's purposes, however, are theological: (1) to show how Christianity stands in relationship to Judaism (see the commentary on 6:8–15); (2) to account for the Jewish persecution of Christian missionaries; (3) to explain why the Temple was destroyed in A.D. 70; (4) to demonstrate that salvation comes from Jesus and not from Temple worship.

Although Stephen's speech is almost unending in its narration of the history of Abraham, Joseph, Moses, David, and Solomon, it omits other heroes of Israel's story like Adam and Eve, King Saul, and the great prophets such as Isaiah. *Why this selective reading of God's covenant history with his people?* Luke's way of handling Israel's history might be likened to our telling our family history and failing to mention our two younger brothers. Why did Luke leave so many Old Testament figures out of Stephen's speech?

A third and final question surfaces. In narrating the stories of Joseph, Moses, David, and Solomon, *why does Stephen say what he does about them and not something else?* Joseph, of whom his brothers were jealous, is a type of Jesus (7:9). Moses, who is both leader and judge (7:35), is a type of Jesus, the prophet raised up by God (7:37; see Ac 3:22–23). His brothers did not realize that through Moses (Jesus) God would liberate them (7:25). David and Solomon are singled out for their role in the construction of God's house, where God does not live (7:48). Among the multitudinous details the Old Testament contains about each of these figures, why does Luke select those he does?

Luke's selective reading of the Old Testament in Stephen's speech is his way of sharing a secret with his readers. Luke is like a person who shares with a friend the meaning of the recent death of a loved one. That death has smashed open the present and is compelling the bereaved to question the past. The past takes on new significance. Past events are rearranged into new configurations. What was once insignificant is now primal and vice versa. Joy and sorrow vie for dominance as the events of the past tumble through one's consciousness. The past causes the present to blossom with lush meaning or else to be darkened by an ominously black cloud.

In Stephen's speech Luke bares his soul for his readers. He beckons them to look at the meaning of Jesus' rejection and death (7:52) from the vantage point of how God dealt with his people in the past and how they rejected him (7:42–43). He shares with them his way of interpreting the recent destruction of the Temple. The people have been prone to unworthy worship from the beginning of God's covenant relationship with them. Temple worship, moreover, would never save; only Jesus saves (see 7:39–43, 48–50; also 4:12). Luke warns his readers that there are joyful and painful ways of reading the history of God's past deal-

ings with his people. In joy Luke recounts the bountiful
riches God has lavished on his covenant partners
(7:5–8). In sorrow Luke rehearses how God's people have tended to worship him in an unworthy manner
and have been against his prophets (7:51–53). Not all
the Jews who hear the missionaries of Luke's community preach that Jesus is God's present gift to his people,
will respond positively to that message. They can be
likened to people who reject a friend's sharing of the
meaning of the death of a loved one. The intimate sharing of how such a significant event reshaped the friend's
past invites the listener to question his own past. The
listener may not rejoice in engaging in such a turbulent
project, may turn his friend off, and may even flee the
friendship.

Luke has shared his secret with us. Jesus—God's
spokesman, rejected by the Jews, God's leader and redeemer, preached among the Jews as the only means of
salvation—this Jesus provides Luke with the eyes
through which he can understand the meaning of God's
call and Israel's response in the past and in the present.

STUDY QUESTION: Luke found the answer to questions
which agitated his community by
pondering the scriptures. Is that
route open to us today?

Acts 7:54 to 8:3
TAKE COURAGE—FROM DEATH
COMES LIFE

54 They were infuriated when they heard this, and ground their teeth at him.

55 But Stephen, filled with the Holy Spirit, gazed into heaven and saw the glory of God, and Jesus
56 standing at God's right hand. ·"I can see heaven thrown open," he said, "and the Son of Man
57 standing at the right hand of God." ·At this all the members of the council shouted out and stopped their ears with their hands; then they all rushed at
58 him, ·sent him out of the city and stoned him. The witnesses put down their clothes at the feet of a
59 young man called Saul. ·As they were stoning him, Stephen said in invocation, "Lord Jesus, receive
60 my spirit." ·Then he knelt down and said aloud, "Lord, do not hold this sin against them"; and
1 with these words he fell asleep. **8** Saul entirely approved of the killing.

That day a bitter persecution started against the church in Jerusalem and everyone except the apostles fled to the country districts of Judaea and Samaria.

2 There were some devout people, however, who buried Stephen and made great mourning for him.

3 Saul then worked for the total destruction of the Church; he went from house to house arresting both men and women and sending them to prison.

✠

This section is like a complex intersection. We can keep our directions straight if we single out three landmarks: (1) Stephen, model of courage and hope; (2) Saul, fierce persecutor now, outstanding missionary later; (3) the apostles, who remain in Jerusalem.

Stephen is Spirit-filled (6:5), one of the prophets who are persecuted (see 7:52). But Stephen is much more. His martyrdom is modeled after that of Jesus. Stephen's "Lord Jesus, receive my spirit" (7:59) is comparable to Jesus' "Father, into your hands I commit my spirit" (Lk 23:46). Stephen's "Lord, do not hold this sin against them" (7:60) is closely parallel to Jesus' "Father, forgive them; they do not know what they are doing" (Lk 23:34). But Stephen is not just a model; he is hope personified for missionaries in a similar situation. These individuals may draw hope from Stephen that their staunch confession of Jesus will be blessed with a similar vision of the Son of Man and a share in his glory. The gift of this vision and glory fulfills Jesus' promise: "I tell you, if anyone openly declares himself for me in the presence of men, the Son of Man will declare himself for him in the presence of God's angels" (Lk 12:8; see also Lk 6:22–23 and 22:69).

With the mention of Saul (7:58; 8:1a, 3) Stephen's persecutors exit from the stage. Saul becomes the epitome of the persecutor (see also Ac 22:20 and 26:9–11). But God will call this violent persecutor to be the greatest missionary in the history of the primitive church and thus will fulfill his promise of salvation for all nations (see further Ac 22:21 and 26:17–18). It should also be noted that missionary expansion is the fruit of persecution. See how Acts 8:4 and 11:19—missionary expansion to Samaria and Antioch respectively —refer back to the onslaught of persecution mentioned in 8:1.

The apostles remain in Jerusalem (8:1). This seems highly unlikely historically. Persecutors, especially the systematic Saul (8:3), would have pursued the leaders of the Christian movement, who would be easy prey in Jerusalem. By arranging that the apostles remain in Jerusalem, Luke underscores the fact that they form the bond of continuity with Judaism and that from Jerusalem they will oversee the expansion of the church. See Acts 8:14: "When the apostles in Jerusalem heard that Samaria had accepted the word of God, they sent Peter and John to them."

This section concludes the Jerusalem phase of Acts and is the beginning of the missionary expansion of the church beyond Jerusalem (see the commentary on 1:8). As a conclusion, it climaxes some earlier themes. In chapters 1 through 7 Luke's intent has not been to chronicle the history of the primitive church, but to reassure his beleaguered missionary communities of God's fidelity to his promises. Individual points in this assurance are that through the twelve apostles the church stands in continuity with Jesus, that the church stands in continuity with Judaism, whose leaders have rejected Jesus and seem prone to reject Jesus' missionaries, that Jesus and he alone is necessary for salvation, and that opposition and persecution do not spell death but engender life.

STUDY QUESTION: How can the Spirit-filled Stephen serve as a model for Christians today?

The Mission Expands to Samaria
Acts 8:4 to 9:43

Acts 8:4–25
THE SPIRIT RATIFIES MISSIONARY EXPANSION

⁴ Those who had escaped went from place to
⁵ place preaching the Good News. ·One of them
was Philip who went to a Samaritan town and
⁶ proclaimed the Christ to them. ·The people united
in welcoming the message Philip preached, either
because they had heard of the miracles he worked
⁷ or because they saw them for themselves. ·There
were, for example, unclean spirits that came
shrieking out of many who were possessed, and
⁸ several paralytics and cripples were cured. ·As a
result there was great rejoicing in that town.
⁹ Now a man called Simon had already practiced
magic arts in the town and astounded the Samaritan people. He had given it out that he was some-
¹⁰ one momentous, ·and everyone believed what he
said; eminent citizens and ordinary people alike
had declared, "He is the divine power that is
¹¹ called Great." ·They had only been won over to
him because of the long time he had spent working
¹² on them with his magic. ·But when they believed
Philip's preaching of the Good News about the
kingdom of God and the name of Jesus Christ,
¹³ they were baptized, both men and women, ·and
even Simon himself became a believer. After his
baptism Simon, who went around constantly with
Philip, was astonished when he saw the wonders
and great miracles that took place.
¹⁴ When the apostles in Jerusalem heard that Samaria had accepted the word of God, they sent
¹⁵ Peter and John to them, ·and they went down
there, and prayed for the Samaritans to receive
¹⁶ the Holy Spirit, ·for as yet he had not come down
on any of them: they had only been baptized in

17 the name of the Lord Jesus. ·Then they laid hands on them, and they received the Holy Spirit.

18 When Simon saw that the Spirit was given through the imposition of hands by the apostles,
19 he offered them some money. ·"Give me the same power," he said, "so that anyone I lay my hands
20 on will receive the Holy Spirit." ·Peter answered, "May your silver be lost forever, and you with it, for thinking that money could buy what God has
21 given for nothing! ·You have no share, no rights, in this: God can see how your heart is warped.
22 Repent of this wickedness of yours, and pray to the Lord; you may still be forgiven for thinking
23 as you did; ·it is plain to me that you are trapped in
24 the bitterness of gall and the chains of sin." ·"Pray to the Lord for me yourselves," Simon replied, "so that none of the things you have spoken about may happen to me."
25 Having given their testimony and proclaimed the word of the Lord, they went back to Jerusalem, preaching the Good News to a number of Samaritan villages.

✠

Recently I saw a play. There were four characters. One was complex and the center of attraction. The other three played minor but important roles. This section is like that play. One message dominates and makes its complex point by interacting with three undeveloped messages. Let's begin with the three minor messages.

First, the missionary expansion described in this section fulfills Jesus' promise: "you will be my witnesses not only in Jerusalem but throughout Judaea and *Samaria* . . ." (1:8). Furthermore, expansion into Samaria is among "outcast" people. Samaritans, who were half Jew and half pagan and who esteemed only the Pentateuch as scripture, were held in low regard by the Jews. "Jews, in fact, do not associate with Samaritans" (Jn 4:9). As is his wont, Luke shows how the gospel is welcomed by outcasts.

The second theme is that Christianity is victorious over magic, one of the most powerful forces over people in antiquity (see 8:11). God's working through Philip wins over Simon the magician (8:13). Simon also realizes that the Spirit, which the apostles mediate, far surpasses all his spells, incantations, and secret formulae (8:18–19). Christianity's superiority over magic is also highlighted in Acts 13:4–12 and 19:11–19.

The third theme is closely related to the preceding one. As one reads between the lines of 8:17–24, it becomes clear that Simon works his magic for money. Simon's attempt to buy the power of bestowing the Spirit is fittingly condemned, and is the origin of the word "simony." Simon serves as a negative example for missionaries and leaders in Luke's community. They should not put God's free gift (8:20) on the money market and use their ministry for self-aggrandizement.

The major and complex theme of this section revolves around 8:14–17 and has been the subject of intense discussion. Some questions in the discussion are: Is this passage a proof text for the sacrament of confirmation? Is Spirit-baptism superior to water-baptism? Answers to these vexed questions are not easily found, but the following points will lead to reasonable solutions.

Philip's role in the spread of the gospel to Samaria is minimalized. He cannot impart the Holy Spirit. The mother church in Jerusalem through its apostles Peter and John perform that vitally important ministry. Their laying on of hands (8:17) demonstrates their authority and says little about either baptism or confirmation (see the commentary on 6:1–7). Luke describes three manifestations of the Holy Spirit: (1) a gift which every Christian receives at baptism (e.g., 2:38); (2) an endowment for Christian leaders which enables them to accomplish specific tasks (e.g., Philip in 8:29 and 39, and Paul in 9:17, 13:9, and 20:23); (3) a guide for the church in its mission. The third type of manifestation of the Spirit is evident in this section. Luke demonstrates that the Holy Spirit ratifies missionary expansion into a foreign territory like Samaria by indicating that the Samaritans receive the gift of tongues—glossalalia. This seems to be the correct interpretation of 8:18. How else could Simon see that the Spirit was given if the gift of the Spirit were not externally manifest? And we know from parallel passages in 10:44–46, where the Spirit ratifies Peter's mission to the pagan Cornelius, and in 19:6, where the Spirit ratifies Paul's mission to disciples of John the Baptist, that the Spirit manifested his presence externally through the phenomenon of speaking in tongues.

One final point. Peter's role in this section overshadows that of John (see especially 8:20–24) and sets up a parallel with and anticipates the function of Paul in 19:1–7. Note the parallels between 8:4–25 and 19:1–7: Philip, a nonapostle, makes room for Peter and John—Apollos, a nonapostle, makes room for Paul, the outstanding missionary; Peter brings the Samaritans into union with the mother church in Jerusalem—Paul brings the disciples of John the Baptist into union with the Ephesian missionary church; Peter combats the magician Simon—Paul combats the Jewish exorcists (19:11–19). Paul is equivalent to Peter, for both have power to bestow the full measure of God's gifts to disciples.

In summary, this section is not a proof text for confirmation nor does it teach the superiority of Spirit-baptism over water-baptism. The external manifestation of the Spirit is Luke's way of showing: (1) how

the spread of Christianity is dependent on the founda-
tional church in Jerusalem and its apostles, and (2)
that the Spirit ratifies the church's missionary expansion.

STUDY QUESTION: In this section Luke seems to be
saying that the Spirit is controlled
by the institutional church, which
dispenses it to whomsoever it wills.
What, then, is the role of the prophets whom God raises up to challenge the institutional church?

CHRISTIANITY MOVES INTO AFRICA

26 The angel of the Lord spoke to Philip saying, "Be ready to set out at noon along the road that goes from Jerusalem down to Gaza, the desert 27 road." ·So he set off on his journey. Now it happened that an Ethiopian had been on pilgrimage to Jerusalem; he was a eunuch and an officer at the court of the kandake, or queen, of Ethiopia, 28 and was in fact her chief treasurer. ·He was now on his way home; and as he sat in his chariot he 29 was reading the prophet Isaiah. ·The Spirit said to 30 Philip, "Go up and meet that chariot." ·When Philip ran up, he heard him reading Isaiah the prophet and asked, "Do you understand what you 31 are reading?" ·"How can I," he replied, "unless I have someone to guide me?" So he invited Philip 32 to get in and sit by his side. ·Now the passage of scripture he was reading was this:

Like a sheep that is led to the slaughterhouse,
like a lamb that is dumb in front of its shearers,
like these he never opens his mouth.
33 He has been humiliated and has no one to defend him.
Who will ever talk about his descendants,
since his life on earth has been cut short!

34 The eunuch turned to Philip and said, "Tell me, is the prophet referring to himself or someone 35 else?" ·Starting, therefore, with this text of scripture Philip proceeded to explain the Good News of Jesus to him.
36 Further along the road they came to some water, and the eunuch said, "Look, there is some water here; is there anything to stop me being bap-38 tized? ·He ordered the chariot to stop, then Philip

and the eunuch both went down into the water
39 and Philip baptized him. ·But after they had come
up out of the water again Philip was taken away
by the Spirit of the Lord, and the eunuch never
saw him again but went on his way rejoicing.
40 Philip found that he had reached Azotus and continued his journey proclaiming the Good News in
every town as far as Caesarea.

✠

This story is a diamond in the rough, which Luke
seems to have had neither time nor interest to polish.
Let's see whether we can spot some of its brilliance.

Although the term "eunuch" (8:37) need not imply
that this highly placed official was castrated, it seems
that Luke takes him to be such. Like Samaritans (see
8:4-25), the eunuch was an outcast. See Deuteronomy
23:1-2: "A man whose testicles have been crushed or
whose male member has been cut off is not to be ad-
mitted to the assembly of Yahweh." Also see Isaiah
56:3-7 where covenant-observant eunuchs are promised an everlasting namc. Through this story Luke is
saying that the eunuch's outcast status does not hinder
him from participating in the Christian assembly
(8:36).

At the hands of Philip, whose commission came
from the Jerusalem apostles (see 6:1-7), Christianity
enters Africa. The mission to Africa is also fully determined by God, who arranges all the odd sets of circum-
stances which dot this story—for example, the eunuch
just happens to be reading a suffering-servant poem
from Isaiah as Philip meets the chariot.

In brief, the Christian message continues to spread
after persecution. This time it moves into Africa. Nothing more is said in Acts about the eunuch's conversion,
which is only remotely supervised by the apostles in

Jerusalem. In contrast to 8:4–25, where the institutional church almost controls the Spirit, this story loudly proclaims that the Spirit blows where it wills.

STUDY QUESTION: Can you think of any reason why Luke simply displays the diamond of this section without first polishing it?

Acts 9:1–19
SAUL, PERSECUTOR TURNED
MISSIONARY, BY THE CALL OF GOD

9 ¹ Meanwhile Saul was still breathing threats to slaughter the Lord's disciples. He had gone to ² the high priest ·and asked for letters addressed to the synagogues in Damascus, that would authorize him to arrest and take to Jerusalem any followers of the Way, men or women, that he could find.

³ Suddenly, while he was traveling to Damascus and just before he reached the city, there came a ⁴ light from heaven all around him. ·He fell to the ground, and then he heard a voice saying, "Saul, ⁵ Saul, why are you persecuting me?" ·"Who are you, Lord?" he asked, and the voice answered, "I ⁶ am Jesus, and you are persecuting me. ·Get up now and go into the city, and you will be told what ⁷ you have to do." ·The men traveling with Saul stood there speechless, for though they heard the ⁸ voice they could see no one. ·Saul got up from the ground, but even with his eyes wide open he could see nothing at all, and they had to lead him into ⁹ Damascus by the hand. ·For three days he was without his sight, and took neither food nor drink.

¹⁰ A disciple called Ananias who lived in Damascus had a vision in which he heard the Lord say to him, "Ananias!" When he replied, "Here I am, ¹¹ Lord," ·the Lord said, "You must go to Straight Street and ask at the house of Judas for someone called Saul, who comes from Tarsus. At this mo-¹² ment he is praying, ·having had a vision of a man called Ananias coming in and laying hands on him to give him back his sight."

¹³ When he heard that, Ananias said, "Lord, several people have told me about this man and all the harm he has been doing to your saints in Jeru-

14 salem. ·He has only come here because he holds a warrant from the chief priests to arrest everybody
15 who invokes your name." ·The Lord replied, "You must go all the same, because this man is my chosen instrument to bring my name before pagans and pagan kings and before the people of
16 Israel; ·I myself will show him how much he him-
17 self must suffer for my name." ·Then Ananias went. He entered the house, and at once laid his hands on Saul and said, "Brother Saul, I have been sent by the Lord Jesus who appeared to you on your way here so that you may recover your sight
18 and be filled with the Holy Spirit." ·Immediately it was as though scales fell away from Saul's eyes and he could see again. So he was baptized there
19 and then, ·and after taking some food he regained his strength.

✠

After depicting missionary expansion to outcasts in 8:4–40, Luke now resumes his account of Saul (see 8:3). He will interrupt that account again from 9:30 to 11:18 with the story of the apostle Peter's conversion of the first gentile, Cornelius. Once the mission to the gentiles has been authenticated by God's action in an apostle, Luke will devote almost the entire remainder of Acts to Saul, renamed Paul, *the* missionary to the gentiles (11:25 to 28:30).

This section is anything but a simple story of how Saul was knocked off his horse and converted. Our popular religious imagination and art to the contrary notwithstanding, this section and its parallels in 22:1–16 and 26:9–18 nowhere say that he was riding a horse. Nor do these texts speak of Saul's conversion as if he were the most wretched sinner antiquity sired. This section is a "vocation" story. We will mine the rich vein of this vocation story on three levels: (1)

Saul as persecutor; (2) Saul's vocation; (3) Luke's intentions and the figure of Paul.

Saul as persecutor. From what Luke says in Acts it
is patent that Saul is not a private persecutor; he repre-
sents official Judaism. This factor is present in all three
accounts of Saul's call: 9:1–3; 22:4–5, 19; 26:9–11.
Since this last passage is the climax of Luke's description of this point, it bears quoting in full here: "As for
me, I once thought it was my duty to use every means
to oppose the name of Jesus the Nazarene. This I did in
Jerusalem; I myself threw many of the saints into
prison, *acting on authority from the chief priests,* and
when they were sentenced to death I cast my vote
against them. I often went around the synagogues
inflicting penalties, trying in this way to force them to
renounce their faith; my fury against them was so extreme that I even pursued them into foreign cities." In
describing Saul as an archpersecutor of the church,
Luke is in accord with the self-portrait Paul paints in
his epistles. See Galatians 1:13: "You must have heard
of my career as a practicing Jew, how merciless I was
in persecuting the Church of God, how much damage I
did to it" (note also Ga 1:23; Ph 3:6; 1 Co 15:9).

Saul's vocation. Saul would never have changed from
awesome persecutor of the Lord's disciples to tireless
missionary to the gentiles unless the Lord had called
him. In what must have taken more time than the three
accounts of Acts lead us to believe, Saul lets the Lord's
call to him sink into and under his persecutor skin.
That call is voiced in 9:15; 22:14, 21; 26:16–18. Acts
9:15 gives a streamlined version of the call: "this man
is my chosen instrument to bring my name before pagans and pagan kings and before the people of Israel."
Luke's version of Saul's call resonates well with Paul's
personal description: "Then God, who had specially
chosen me while I was still in my mother's womb,

called me through his grace and chose to reveal his Son in me, so that I might preach the Good News about him to the pagans" (Ga 1:15–16). The story of Saul, persecutor turned missionary, edifies Luke's community: God does preserve his church from persecution; encouragement is offered to those who suffer persecution like that directed by and enfleshed in Saul.

Luke's intentions and the figure of Paul. A question may help us peer into Luke's threefold intention in this section: Why does Luke have three accounts of Paul's call? First, by devoting precious space to three accounts of Paul's call, Luke spotlights the significance of Paul at key points in his story. In chapter 9 the call of the missionary to the gentiles par excellence—Paul—is introduced when the Spirit is on the brink of moving the mission to the gentiles (see 10:1–48). In chapters 22 and 26 the call of Paul is introduced to show that Paul and Christianity are not apostates from Judaism; both Jews and Romans should take careful note that Christianity fulfills the promises God gave to Judaism. Second, Luke highlights the fact that the mission to the gentiles was not due to human caprice; God willed it in fulfillment of his promises. This fulfillment is embodied in the very person of Paul (for more detail on how Paul embodies the fulfillment of God's promises, see the commentary on 26:16–18). Finally, Luke's intent is to supply ammunition for his communities, some of which have been founded by Paul and are under attack from Jews because of their faith. Luke tells them that through Paul, once an observant Pharisee and merciless persecutor of the church, they stand in continuity with Judaism. Like Paul, they are not apostates from Judaism. Like Paul, they have had their eyes opened by God to see that Judaism is fulfilled in Jesus. See the commentaries on 22:1–29 and 26:1–32 for further data on Luke's purpose for narrating Paul's call thrice.

STUDY QUESTIONS: Does the story of Saul's call tell us anything about our call to be Christians? Does a call or "conversion" occur with the rapidity which Luke seems to assign to Saul's?

TWO PORTRAITS OF PAUL

After he had spent only a few days with the 20 disciples in Damascus, ·he began preaching in the 21 synagogues, "Jesus is the Son of God." ·All his hearers were amazed. "Surely," they said, "this is the man who organized the attack in Jerusalem against the people who invoke this name, and who came here for the sole purpose of arresting them 22 to have them tried by the chief priests?" ·Saul's power increased steadily, and he was able to throw the Jewish colony at Damascus into complete confusion by the way he demonstrated that Jesus was the Christ.

23 Some time passed, and the Jews worked out a 24 plot to kill him, ·but news of it reached Saul. To make sure of killing him they kept watch on the 25 gates day and night, ·but when it was dark the disciples took him and let him down from the top of the wall, lowering him in a basket.

26 When he got to Jerusalem he tried to join the disciples, but they were all afraid of him: they 27 could not believe he was really a disciple. ·Barnabas, however, took charge of him, introduced him to the apostles, and explained how the Lord had appeared to Saul and spoken to him on his journey, and how he had preached boldly at Damas- 28 cus in the name of Jesus. ·Saul now started to go around with them in Jerusalem, preaching fear- 29 lessly in the name of the Lord. ·But after he had spoken to the Hellenists, and argued with them, 30 they became determined to kill him. ·When the brothers knew, they took him to Caesarea, and sent him off from there to Tarsus.

31 The churches throughout Judaea, Galilee and Samaria were now left in peace, building them-

selves up, living in the fear of the Lord, and filled
with the consolation of the Holy Spirit.

✠

This section makes one simple point and one exceed-
ingly complex one. The simple point is that God's call
of Saul changed him so radically that people could not
believe their eyes and ears (9:21–22, 26).

The complex point is Saul's appearance in Jerusalem
(9:26). At first blush, this point hardly seems complex,
but when the reader notices what Paul says in Galatians 1–2 about his visits to Jerusalem, problems
abound. The salient portion of Galatians is Paul's saying that, after his call to preach to the pagans, "I did
not stop to discuss this with any human being, nor did I
go up to Jerusalem to see those who were already apostles before me, but *I went off to Arabia at once* and
later went straight back from there to Damascus. Even
when *after three years I went up to Jerusalem* to visit
Cephas and stayed with him for fifteen days, I did not
see any of the other disciples; I only saw James, the
brother of the Lord . . ." (Ga 1:16–19). The problem
surfaces: The Paul of Acts does not seem to be the
same as the Paul of the letters. If we phrase the problem this way, we must immediately beware of looking for black-and-white solutions, as if Luke were
wrong and Paul right. The correct answer should be
sought in the sensitive comparison of what Acts and
Paul say about Paul. Such a process is like contem-
plating two portraits of a great person: Paul paints a
self-portrait, Luke a portrait from a later perspective.
Differences there are, but the similarities outweigh the
differences.

Let's take a brief look at these two portraits. By
bringing Saul to Jerusalem (9:26–30), Luke joins him

immediately to the source of the Christian message, to the bond of continuity between Judaism, Jesus, the twelve apostles, and the church. In this very brief section Luke makes no mention of Paul's Arabian mission (see Ga 1:17; also note that Luke takes no time to give the reader information about how Damascus was evangelized). Paul, for his part, is so eager to defend the independence of his gospel that he relegates the more famous Barnabas to a secondary position (see Ga 2:1, 9, and contrast Ac 9:27; 11:25; 12:1–3). Paul succumbs to the common tendency to telescope one's career; Paul worked in the shadow of Barnabas for many a year and did not become a famous and successful missionary overnight.

When Acts puts Paul in the limelight, we will have occasion to continue the portrait study we have begun here. The reader should bear in mind that to regard one portrait as more true to life than the other does not accord with the reality of this multifaceted and influential missionary.

STUDY QUESTION: Read through the first two chapters of Galatians carefully and compare them with this section. Does Paul present an account of his call and ministry which is irreconcilable with Luke's account?

Acts 9:32–43
THE SPIRIT-FILLED PETER
CONTINUES JESUS' MISSION

32 Peter visited one place after another and eventually came to the saints living down in Lydda. 33 There he found a man called Aeneas, a paralytic 34 who had been bedridden for eight years. ·Peter said to him, "Aeneas, Jesus Christ cures you: get up and fold up your sleeping mat." Aeneas got up 35 immediately; ·everybody who lived in Lydda and Sharon saw him, and they were all converted to the Lord.

36 At Jaffa there was a woman disciple called Tabitha, or Dorcas in Greek, who never tired of 37 doing good or giving in charity. ·But the time came when she got ill and died, and they washed her 38 and laid her out in a room upstairs. ·Lydda is not far from Jaffa, so when the disciples heard that Peter was there, they sent two men with an urgent message for him, "Come and visit us as soon as possible."

39 Peter went back with them straightaway, and on his arrival they took him to the upstairs room, where all the widows stood around him in tears, showing him tunics and other clothes Dorcas had 40 made when she was with them. ·Peter sent them all out of the room and knelt down and prayed. Then he turned to the dead woman and said, "Tabitha, stand up." She opened her eyes, looked 41 at Peter and sat up. ·Peter helped her to her feet, then he called in the saints and widows and 42 showed them she was alive. ·The whole of Jaffa heard about it and many believed in the Lord.

43 Peter stayed on some time in Jaffa, lodging with a leather tanner called Simon.

☩

Whereas earlier in Acts Luke gave just one example
of the miracle-working ability of the apostles (3:1–10)
and presented three generalizations (2:43; 4:33;
5:12), here he devotes space to two full-fledged miracles of Peter. One of his purposes is narrative—i.e., to
have Peter in Jaffa so that Cornelius can summon him
thence (see 10:5–6). His two other purposes are theological.

First, Jesus' mission of making the lame walk and
raising the dead to life (see Lk 7:22) is continued in
the ministry of Peter through the power of Jesus' word
(9:34). As a matter of fact, the two miracles are rather
similar to two of Jesus': the paralytic in Luke 5:18–26
and the daughter of Jairus in 8:40–56. In his description of Peter's second miracle (9:36–42) Luke uses
features from a similar miracle of Elijah, the great Old
Testament miracle-working prophet. Note the word
"upper room" in both Acts 9:37, 39 and 1 Kings
17:19, 23.

Luke's second theological purpose is to emphasize
that the word is spreading throughout Judaea. He does
so in shorthand by underlining miracles as the occa-
sions of faith (see 9:35, 42; also 8:6–8). Obviously
much more was needed than a mere miracle for conversion to occur, but Luke's shorthand leaves him no opportunity for mention of extensive catechesis or even
baptism. He is content to note that the Christian mission continues its expansion beyond Jerusalem.

STUDY QUESTION: Tabitha/Dorcas, the gazelle, is singled out for her almsgiving (9:36,
39). By giving prominence to this
characteristic which is also present

in Cornelius, the hero of the next
section (10:2, 4, 31), is Luke saying that almsgiving is a key to God's
heart?

The Mission Opens Out to the Ends of the Earth
Acts 10:1 to 28:31

Acts 10:1 to 11:18
GENTILES DO NOT HAVE
TO BECOME JEWS TO BE SAVED

¹ **10** One of the centurions of the Italica cohort stationed in Caesarea was called Cornelius.
² He and the whole of his household were devout and God-fearing, and he gave generously to Jewish causes and prayed constantly to God.
³ One day at about the ninth hour he had a vision in which he distinctly saw the angel of God come into his house and call out to him, "Cornelius!"
⁴ He stared at the vision in terror and exclaimed, "What is it, Lord?" "Your offering of prayers and alms," the angel answered, "has been accepted by
⁵ God. ·Now you must send someone to Jaffa and
⁶ fetch a man called Simon, known as Peter, ·who is lodging with Simon the tanner whose house is
⁷ by the sea." ·When the angel who said this had gone, Cornelius called two of the slaves and a de-
⁸ vout soldier of his staff, ·told them what had happened, and sent them off to Jaffa.
⁹ Next day, while they were still on their journey and had only a short distance to go before reaching Jaffa, Peter went to the housetop at about the
¹⁰ sixth hour to pray. ·He felt hungry and was looking forward to his meal, but before it was ready he
¹¹ fell into a trance ·and saw heaven thrown open and something like a big sheet being let down to earth
¹² by its four corners; ·it contained every possible sort of animal and bird, walking, crawling or fly-
¹³ ing ones. ·A voice then said to him, "Now, Peter;
¹⁴ kill and eat!" ·But Peter answered, "Certainly not, Lord; I have never yet eaten anything profane or
¹⁵ unclean." ·Again, a second time, the voice spoke to him, "What God has made clean, you have no
¹⁶ right to call profane." ·This was repeated three

times, and then suddenly the container was drawn
up to heaven again.

17 Peter was still worrying over the meaning of the
vision he had seen, when the men sent by Cornelius arrived. They had asked where Simon's
house was and they were now standing at the
18 door, ·calling out to know if the Simon known as
19 Peter was lodging there. ·Peter's mind was still on
the vision and the Spirit had to tell him, "Some
20 men have come to see you. ·Hurry down, and do
not hesitate about going back with them; it was I
21 who told them to come." ·Peter went down and
said to them, "I am the man you are looking for;
22 why have you come?" ·They said, "The centurion
Cornelius, who is an upright and God-fearing
man, highly regarded by the entire Jewish people,
was directed by a holy angel to send for you and
bring you to his house and to listen to what you
23 have to say." ·So Peter asked them in and gave
them lodging.

Next day, he was ready to go off with them, accompanied by some of the brothers from Jaffa.
24 They reached Caesarea the following day, and
Cornelius was waiting for them. He had asked his
25 relations and close friends to be there, ·and as
Peter reached the house Cornelius went out to
meet him, knelt at his feet and prostrated himself.
26 But Peter helped him up. "Stand up," he said, "I
27 am only a man after all!" ·Talking together they
went in to meet all the people assembled there,
28 and Peter said to them, "You know it is forbidden
for Jews to mix with people of another race and
visit them, but God has made it clear to me that I
29 must not call anyone profane or unclean. ·That is
why I made no objection to coming when I was
sent for; but I should like to know exactly why
30 you sent for me." ·Cornelius replied, "Three days
ago I was praying in my house at the ninth hour,
when I suddenly saw a man in front of me in shin-
31 ing robes. ·He said, 'Cornelius, your prayer has
been heard and your alms have been accepted as
32 a sacrifice in the sight of God; ·so now you must
send to Jaffa and fetch Simon known as Peter who

is lodging in the house of Simon the tanner, by the
³³ sea.' ·So I sent for you at once, and you have been
kind enough to come. Here we all are, assembled
in front of you to hear what message God has
given you for us."

³⁴   Then Peter addressed them: "The truth I have
now come to realize," he said, "is that God does
³⁵ not have favorites, ·but that anybody of any na-
tionality who fears God and does what is right is
acceptable to him.

³⁶   "It is true, God sent his word to the people of
Israel, and it was to them that the good news of
peace was brought by Jesus Christ—but Jesus
³⁷ Christ is Lord of all men. ·You must have heard
about the recent happenings in Judaea; about
Jesus of Nazareth and how he began in Galilee,
³⁸ after John had been preaching baptism. ·God had
anointed him with the Holy Spirit and with power,
and because God was with him, Jesus went about
doing good and curing all who had fallen into the
³⁹ power of the devil. ·Now I, and those with me, can
witness to everything he did throughout the countryside of Judaea and in Jerusalem itself: and also
to the fact that they killed him by hanging him on
⁴⁰ a tree, ·yet three days afterward God raised him
⁴¹ to life and allowed him to be seen, ·not by the
whole people but only by certain witnesses God
had chosen beforehand. Now we are those witnesses—we have eaten and drunk with him after
⁴² his resurrection from the dead—·and he has or-
dered us to proclaim this to his people and to tell
them that God has appointed him to judge every-
⁴³ one, alive or dead. ·It is to him that all the proph-
ets bear this witness: that all who believe in Jesus
will have their sins forgiven through his name."

⁴⁴   While Peter was still speaking the Holy Spirit
⁴⁵ came down on all the listeners. ·Jewish believers
who had accompanied Peter were all astonished
that the gift of the Holy Spirit should be poured
⁴⁶ out on the pagans too, ·since they could hear them
speaking strange languages and proclaiming the
⁴⁷ greatness of God. Peter himself then said, ·"Could
anyone refuse the water of baptism to these peo-

ple, now they have received the Holy Spirit just
48 as much as we have?" ·He then gave orders for
them to be baptized in the name of Jesus Christ.
Afterward they begged him to stay on for some
days.

1   **11** The apostles and the brothers in Judaea
heard that the pagans too had accepted the
2 word of God, ·and when Peter came up to Jeru-
3 salem the Jews criticized him ·and said, "So you
have been visiting the uncircumcised and eating
4 with them, have you?" ·Peter in reply gave them
5 the details point by point: ·"One day, when I was
in the town of Jaffa," he began, "I fell into a
trance as I was praying and had a vision of something like a big sheet being let down from heaven
by its four corners. This sheet reached the ground
6 quite close to me. ·I watched it intently and saw
all sorts of animals and wild beasts—everything
7 possible that could walk, crawl or fly. ·Then I
heard a voice that said to me, 'Now, Peter; kill and
8 eat!' ·But I answered: Certainly not, Lord; nothing profane or unclean has ever crossed my lips.
9 And a second time the voice spoke from heaven,
'What God has made clean, you have no right to
10 call profane.' ·This was repeated three times, before the whole of it was drawn up to heaven again.

11   "Just at that moment, three men stopped outside the house where we were staying; they had
12 been sent from Caesarea to fetch me, ·and the
Spirit told me to have no hesitation about going
back with them. The six brothers here came with
13 me as well, and we entered the man's house. ·He
told us he had seen an angel standing in his house
who said, 'Send to Jaffa and fetch Simon known
14 as Peter; ·he has a message for you that will save
you and your entire household.'

15   "I had scarcely begun to speak when the Holy
Spirit came down on them in the same way as it
16 came on us at the beginning, ·and I remembered
that the Lord had said, 'John baptized with water,
but you will be baptized with the Holy Spirit.'

¹⁷ I realized then that God was giving them the identical thing he gave to us when we believed in the Lord Jesus Christ; and who was I to stand in God's way?"

¹⁸   This account satisfied them, and they gave glory to God. "God," they said, "can evidently grant even the pagans the repentance that leads to life."

✠

If we concentrate on Luke's repetitions, we will be able to wring the message out of this long section. There are six repetitions of major consequence.

Luke begins his description of how the gospel moved "to the ends of the earth" (see 1:8) by telling a story about Cornelius, a centurion (see Lk 7:2–10 for a parallel description of a centurion). Luke emphasizes how devout, generous, and prayerful Cornelius is (10:2, 4, 31). The first gentile to be converted is an exemplary specimen. In his life he bodies forth a Jewish image of a good person: "Prayer with fasting and alms with right conduct are better than riches with iniquity. Better to practice almsgiving than to hoard up gold. Almsgiving saves from death and purges every kind of sin. Those who give alms have their fill of days" (Tb 12:8–9). Care for the poor disposes Cornelius to be open to God's gift of salvation.

The second repetition stresses the fact that God himself led the gentiles into the Christian community. God's direction of events is repeated in different ways in 10:3, 11–16, 19, 22, 30; 11:5–10, 12–13. The mission to the gentiles was not the result of Peter's bootlegging. God—through angels, visions, and the Spirit—steered that mission.

The third repetition deals with the fact that the Christian powers that be are not easily won over to the idea that God would allow pagans to be saved without

first being entered on the Jewish membership rolls. The
statement "And when Peter came up to Jerusalem the
Jews criticized him and said, 'So you have been visiting
the uncircumcised and eating with them, have you?'"
(11:2–3) is not an isolated example of the hard-nosed
discernment of God's action. But once these apostolic
powers that be recognized the handwriting of the Lord
in Peter's action, they gave his action their endorsement
(11:1, 18). Not only was God directing the mission to
the pagans, but his action even passed muster for the
authoritative twelve apostles (see 10:14, 28, 47; 11:1,
18).

The fourth repetition focuses on the references to the
signal importance of Peter's speech. Cornelius' words
"Here we all are, assembled in front of you to hear
what message God has given you for us" (10:33) are
echoed in 10:22 and 11:14. But it should be noted that
Peter's speech is in tension with other parts of the
story. In 10:37 Peter tells his audience that "you must
have heard about the recent happenings in Judaea," yet
there is no reason to believe that Cornelius knew anything about the Christian message. Further, "I had
scarcely begun to speak when the Holy Spirit came
down on them" (11:15) contradicts what is detailed as
happening in 10:34–36. Moreover, the speech doesn't
lead to conversion as in 2:37 ("What must we do,
brothers?") or in the similar speech of Paul in
13:16–41. The Holy Spirit comes directly on the assembled pagans, an event which makes the speech
superfluous.

The fifth repetition occurs in and around the speech
and will help us unearth the most revolutionary message of this section. "God does not have favorites, but
anybody of any nationality who fears God and does
what is right is acceptable to him" (10:34–35; see also
10:28–29) formulates a principle of radical conse-

quences. Jesus, to whom all the prophets witnessed, is the fulfillment of God's promises (10:43). He has brought peace for *all* people, both Jew and gentile and is Lord of *all* (10:36). *All* who believe in him will have their sins forgiven (10:43). Jesus is the judge of *everyone,* alive or dead (10:42). Put in other terms, the pagan does not have to become a Jew to be saved (see Lk 10:25–37 and the commentary in *Invitation to Luke,* pp. 135–38 for a similar principle). Cornelius and other people who fear God and do what is right are acceptable to God (10:35). This repetition also helps us to tackle some of the problems raised in the consideration of repetition number four. Peter's speech in Cornelius' house is Luke's way of interpreting the major event that non-Jews are accepted by God without having to first become Jews. The speech interprets the event, and does not bear the hallmark of tape-recorder fidelity (see the commentary on 2:14–41 for more detail on this factor of Luke's use of speeches).

The sixth repetition concerns table fellowship between Jews and gentiles (10:23, 48; 11:3). The question of table fellowship, however, is not fully handled in this section. It is introduced here to tease the reader into looking forward to a resolution of the problems it raises. The reader will note that the resolution occurs in chapter 15, where the Cornelius event is again repeated.

So far we have seen that Luke is a good teacher as he employs the time-honored principle that repetition is the mother of study. But why does Luke repeat the things he does? Luke's communities, composed of a minority of Jews and a majority of gentiles, are harassed by Jews for claiming that the Messiah Jesus saves both Jew and gentile. This section consoles these harassed Christians, gives them ammunition in their discussions with their Jewish neighbors, and tells gentile Christia⸺

about their origins. Luke does a virtuoso theological juggling act with three truths: (1) God is faithful to the promises he made to his chosen people as the very presence of Jesus and his witnesses trumpets (10:41, 43); (2) Jesus Christ is Lord of all and saves those who believe in him (10:36, 43); (3) good people are acceptable to God (10:34–35). The Christian crowds may cheer Luke's performance, but there's anguish written all over his face. It's the anguish of wrestling with God to discern his will.

STUDY QUESTION: God saves Hindus and Buddhists who do not believe in Jesus. If this is true, why be a Christian?

Acts 11:19–30
CHRISTIANITY EXPANDS
TO THE BIG CITY

19 Those who had escaped during the persecution that happened because of Stephen traveled as far as Phoenicia and Cyprus and Antioch, but they usually proclaimed the message only to Jews.
20 Some of them, however, who came from Cyprus and Cyrene, went to Antioch where they started preaching to the Greeks, proclaiming the Good
21 News of the Lord Jesus to them as well. ·The Lord helped them, and a great number believed and were converted to the Lord.

22 The church in Jerusalem heard about this and
23 they sent Barnabas to Antioch. ·There he could see for himself that God had given grace, and this pleased him, and he urged them all to remain
24 faithful to the Lord with heartfelt devotion; ·for he was a good man, filled with the Holy Spirit and with faith. And a large number of people were won over to the Lord.

25 Barnabas then left for Tarsus to look for Saul,
26 and when he found him he brought him to Antioch. As things turned out they were to live together in that church a whole year, instructing a large number of people. It was at Antioch that the disciples were first called "Christians."

27 While they were there some prophets came
28 down to Antioch from Jerusalem, ·and one of them whose name was Agabus, seized by the Spirit, stood up and predicted that a famine would spread over the whole empire. This in fact happened before the reign of Claudius came to an
29 end. ·The disciples decided to send relief, each to contribute what he could afford, to the brothers

³⁰ living in Judaea. ·They did this and delivered their
   contributions to the elders in the care of Barnabas
   and Saul.

☩

This section is highly compact. We move from the
four clear points of this section to its two less-clear
points.

First, it is very clear that, by expanding to Antioch,
Christianity has moved into the cosmopolitan world.
Antioch, on the Orontes River in Syria, might be likened in size and importance to Atlanta, Georgia.
After Rome and Alexandria, it was the Roman Empire's largest city, with a population of a half million.
Josephus, the first-century A.D. Jewish historian, describes Antioch: "But it was at Antioch that the Jewish
race specially congregated, partly owing to the greatness of that city, but mainly because the successors of
King Antiochus had enabled them to live there in security. . . . his successors . . . granted them citizen
rights on an equality with the Greeks. . . . the Jewish
colony grew in numbers. . . . they were constantly at-
tracting to their religious ceremonies multitudes of
Greeks, and these they had in some measure incorporated with themselves" (*Jewish War* VII, 43–45, Loeb
translation). By its missionary success in Antioch,
Christianity had moved out of the backwaters into the
big city.

Second, the mother church in Jerusalem sends the
Spirit-filled and highly regarded Barnabas, who gives
his stamp of approval to this missionary expansion and
does not demand circumcision of the pagans before
they can become Christians (11:22–24).

Third, the believers are first called "Christians" or
"followers of the Messiah" by the pagans in Antioch.

By this label the pagans are able to distinguish between Christians and Jews. As we have noted—e.g., in the commentary on 10:1 to 11:18—such a separation from the people of the promises can create problems of continuity with the God of the promises for Luke and his communities.

Fourth, in 11:30 Luke mentions Christian elders for the first time in Acts. This foreshadows the shift in the organization of the church in Jerusalem. The unique group of twelve apostles, based on the model of the twelve patriarchs, is giving way to the synagogue model of elders presided over by one person. See Acts 15:22, where the two models coexist. Note 21:17–19, where the church order of elders with James at the helm has taken over.

There are two less clear points in this compact section. First, 11:19 refers back to 8:1 and is Luke's way of linking the mission to the pagans in Antioch with the flow of his story. He does this, however, at the expense of some inconsistencies. All except the apostles are said to have fled Jerusalem (8:1), yet there are disciples in Jerusalem who can send Barnabas to Antioch (11:22; see also the troublesome 9:26). Luke seems to have painted himself into a corner to preserve his theological scheme that missionary expansion results from persecution.

Second, the commentary on 9:20–31 noted that there are two portraits of Paul in the New Testament: that of Luke in Acts and that of Paul in his letters. In 11:27–30 we encounter this dual portraiture again. Acts 11:27–30 is Luke's description of Paul's second visit to Jerusalem. Paul in Galatians 2:1 gives a different version: "It was not till fourteen years had passed that I went up to Jerusalem again" (see also Ga 1:21–22). Paul in Romans 15:25–28 (cf. Ga 2:10) places the collection for the Jerusalem poor much later in his missionary career. It seems that Luke puts the collection here—at the beginning of the pagan mission—to dramatize the solidarity between the mother church in Jerusalem and the daughter church in Antioch. Because he has placed the collection earlier in his story, he merely hints at the collection which Paul delivered on his final visit to Jerusalem (see 24:17).

STUDY QUESTIONS: Is it progress or regression that Christians move from the small town of Jerusalem to the big city of Antioch? Will Christians be able to preserve the purity of the gospel in such a cosmopolitan setting? By rubbing shoulders with people of different cultures, will Christian missionaries be able to see what is time-conditioned in their presentation of the gospel?

Acts 12:1–25
GOD CARES FOR HIS OWN

¹ 12 It was about this time that King Herod started persecuting certain members of the ² Church. ·He beheaded James the brother of John, ³ and when he saw that this pleased the Jews he ⁴ decided to arrest Peter as well. ·This was during the days of Unleavened Bread, and he put Peter in prison, assigning four squads of four soldiers each to guard him in turns. Herod meant to try Peter in public after the end of Passover week. ⁵ All the time Peter was under guard the Church prayed to God for him unremittingly.

⁶ On the night before Herod was to try him, Peter was sleeping between two soldiers, fastened with double chains, while guards kept watch at the ⁷ main entrance to the prison. ·Then suddenly the angel of the Lord stood there, and the cell was filled with light. He tapped Peter on the side and woke him. "Get up!" he said. "Hurry!"—and the ⁸ chains fell from his hands. ·The angel then said, "Put on your belt and sandals." After he had done this, the angel next said, "Wrap your cloak around ⁹ you and follow me." ·Peter followed him, but had no idea that what the angel did was all happening in reality; he thought he was seeing a vi- ¹⁰ sion. ·They passed through two guard posts one after the other, and reached the iron gate leading to the city. This opened of its own accord; they went through it and had walked the whole length of one street when suddenly the angel left him. ¹¹ It was only then that Peter came to himself. "Now I know it is all true," he said. "The Lord really did send his angel and has saved me from Herod and from all that the Jewish people were so certain would happen to me."

12 As soon as he realized this he went straight to the house of Mary the mother of John Mark, where a number of people had assembled and
13 were praying. ·He knocked at the outside door and a servant called Rhoda came to answer it.
14 She recognized Peter's voice and was so overcome with joy that, instead of opening the door, she ran inside with the news that Peter was standing at
15 the main entrance. ·They said to her, "You are out of your mind," but she insisted that it was
16 true. Then they said, "It must be his angel!" ·Peter, meanwhile, was still knocking, so they opened the door and were amazed to see that it really was
17 Peter himself. ·With a gesture of his hand he stopped them talking, and described to them how the Lord had led him out of prison. He added, "Tell James and the brothers." Then he left and went to another place.
18 When daylight came there was a great commotion among the soldiers, who could not imagine
19 what had become of Peter. ·Herod put out an unsuccessful search for him; he had the guards questioned, and before leaving Judaea to take up residence in Caesarea he gave orders for their execution.
20 Now Herod was on bad terms with the Tyrians and Sidonians. However, they sent a joint deputation which managed to enlist the support of Blastus, the king's chamberlain, and through him negotiated a treaty, since their country depended
21 for its food supply on King Herod's territory. ·A day was fixed, and Herod, wearing his robes of state and enthroned on a dais, made a speech to
22 them. ·The people acclaimed him with, "It is a
23 god speaking, not a man!", ·and at that moment the angel of the Lord struck him down, because he had not given the glory to God. He was eaten away with worms and died.
24 The word of God continued to spread and
25 to gain followers. ·Barnabas and Saul completed their task and came back from Jerusalem, bringing John Mark with them.

✠

Stephen has been stoned (7:58); James has been beheaded (12:2). Does God really care for his persecuted preachers, missionaries, and apostles? In this section Luke answers that faith-testing question with a loud, "Yes, he does!"

The story of Peter's angelically contrived and escorted prison break placards God's concern for his own (see the commentary on 5:17–42). All the cards were stacked against Peter; there was absolutely no human way in which he could have escaped from prison (12:6–10). Even his fellow Christians, although praying unremittingly (12:5), could hardly believe their ears and eyes (12:14–17).

But granted that Peter's liberation from prison symbolizes God's care for his own, what is the fate of those who imprison God's people? A comparison of accounts by Josephus, the first-century A.D. Jewish historian, and by Luke will provide an answer. Josephus' account of Herod Agrippa's last days runs: "On the second day of the spectacles [in honor of Caesar], clad in a garment woven completely of silver . . . he entered the theatre at daybreak. There the silver, illumined by the touch of the first rays of the sun, was wondrously radiant and by its glitter inspired fear and awe in those who gazed intently on it. Straightway his flatterers raised their voices from various directions . . . addressing him as a god. . . . The king did not rebuke them nor did he reject their flattery as impious" (*Jewish Antiquities,* XIX, 344–46, Loeb translation). Josephus continues and says that shortly after the flattery Herod experienced severe abdominal pain which caused him to repent of the folly of accepting such flattery as truth. He died five days later—presumably from a ruptured appendix and not from an angel's blow.

Luke's account is different as Luke goes out of his way to demonstrate that Herod meets the pitiful death reserved for a persecutor of God's people (12:23). Because Herod had persecuted the church, "he had not given the glory to God." Being "eaten away with worms" is the stock fate of those who harass God's people: "He [Antiochus Epiphanes] who only a little while before had thought in his superhuman boastfulness to command the waves of the sea, he who imagined he could weigh mountain peaks in a balance, found himself flat on the ground, borne in a litter, a visible demonstration to all of the power of God, in that the very eyes of this godless man *teemed with worms* and his flesh rotted away while he lingered on in agonizing pain, and the stench of his decay sickened the whole army" (2 M 9:8–9).

God does care for his own and liberates them from their persecutors.

STUDY QUESTION: In his Gospel and Acts Luke has two different views on persecution: (1) persecution thrives and the toll of martyrs rises (Lk 17:20 to 18:8; Lk 23:1–56; Ac 7:54 to 8:3); (2) God miraculously delivers his people from their persecutors (Ac 5:17–42 and here). Are these views contradictory or two sides of the same coin?

1 13 In the church at Antioch the following were prophets and teachers: Barnabas, Simeon called Niger, and Lucius of Cyrene, Manaen, who had been brought up with Herod the tetrarch,
2 and Saul. ·One day while they were offering worship to the Lord and keeping a fast, the Holy Spirit said, "I want Barnabas and Saul set apart for the
3 work to which I have called them." ·So it was that after fasting and prayer they laid their hands on them and sent them off.

4 So these two, sent on their mission by the Holy Spirit, went down to Seleucia and from there
5 sailed to Cyprus. ·They landed at Salamis and proclaimed the word of God in the synagogues of the Jews; John acted as their assistant.

6 They traveled the whole length of the island, and at Paphos they came in contact with a Jewish
7 magician called Bar-jesus. ·This false prophet was one of the attendants of the proconsul Sergius Paulus who was an extremely intelligent man. The proconsul summoned Barnabas and Saul and
8 asked to hear the word of God, ·but Elymas Magos—as he was called in Greek—tried to stop them so as to prevent the proconsul's conversion
9 to the faith. ·Then Saul, whose other name is Paul,
10 looked him full in the face ·and said, "You utter fraud, you impostor, you son of the devil, you enemy of all true religion, why don't you stop twisting the straightforward ways of the Lord?
11 Now watch how the hand of the Lord will strike you: you will be blind, and for a time you will not see the sun." That instant, everything went misty and dark for him, and he groped about to

¹² find someone to lead him by the hand. ·The pro-
consul, who had watched everything, became a
believer, being astonished by what he had learned
about the Lord.

✠

This section has two parts: 13:1–3 and 13:4–12; it
revolves around the theme that the church in Antioch—
itself a daughter church (see the commentary on
11:19–30)—becomes a mother church by sending out
missionaries.

In 13:1–3 it is clear that the church in the cosmopolitan Antioch goes on mission because this is God's
will revealed at prayer: "I want Barnabas and Saul set
apart for the work to which I have called them"
(13:2). In passing, it might be noted that Antioch has
church leaders called by titles not previously mentioned in Acts: prophets and teachers (see the list of
leaders in 1 Co 12:28). Acts has presented a variety of
church leaders: the twelve apostles, the Seven (6:1–7),
and the elders (11:30).

Acts 13:4–12 dramatizes (1) the strategy of the
mission, (2) the opposition leveled at the mission, and
(3) the success of the mission (this mission, usually
called Paul's first missionary journey, continues
through 14:28). "Proclaimed the word of God in the
synagogues of the Jews" enunciates the missionary
strategy and becomes a refrain in 13:5, 14; 14:1;
16:13; 17:1–2, 10, 17; 18:4, 19; 19:8. The mission
will be opposed by Jews (13:6); it will conquer the opposition of magic (13:6, 8; see the commentary on
8:4–25). The mission will be successful as the conversion of a pagan, a most highly placed Roman official,
symbolizes.

Luke now places Paul front and center stage in his

story (see 13:9). Paul is on his way to becoming the great missionary to the gentiles.

STUDY QUESTION: Why does Luke give such prominence to prayer in his account of how the church at Antioch decided to become missionary?

Acts 13:13–52
PAUL, LIKE PETER, CONTINUES
JESUS' MISSION

¹³ Paul and his friends went by sea from Paphos
to Perga in Pamphylia where John left them to
¹⁴ go back to Jerusalem. ·The others carried on from
Perga till they reached Antioch in Pisidia. Here
they went to synagogue on the sabbath and took
¹⁵ their seats. ·After the lessons from the Law and
the Prophets had been read, the presidents of the
synagogue sent them a message: "Brothers, if you
would like to address some words of encourage-
¹⁶ ment to the congregation, please do so." ·Paul
stood up, held up a hand for silence and began
to speak:

¹⁷ "Men of Israel, and fearers of God, listen! ·The
God of our nation Israel chose our ancestors, and
made our people great when they were living as
foreigners in Egypt; then by divine power he led
¹⁸ them out, ·and for about forty years took care of
¹⁹ them in the wilderness. ·When he had destroyed
seven nations in Canaan, he put them in posses-
²⁰ sion of their land ·for about four hundred and fifty
years. After this he gave them judges, down to the
²¹ prophet Samuel. ·Then they demanded a king,
and God gave them Saul son of Kish, a man of
²² the tribe of Benjamin. After forty years, ·he de-
posed him and made David their king, of whom
he approved in these words, 'I have selected David son of Jesse, a man after my own heart, who
²³ will carry out my whole purpose.' ·To keep his
promise, God has raised up for Israel one of Da-
²⁴ vid's descendants, Jesus, as Savior, ·whose coming
was heralded by John when he proclaimed a baptism of repentance for the whole people of Israel.
²⁵ Before John ended his career he said, 'I am not
the one you imagine me to be; that one is coming

after me and I am not fit to undo his sandal.'

26   "My brothers, sons of Abraham's race, and all
you who fear God, this message of salvation is
27   meant for you. ·What the people of Jerusalem and
their rulers did, though they did not realize it,
was in fact to fulfill the prophecies read on every
28   sabbath. ·Though they found nothing to justify his
death, they condemned him and asked Pilate to
29   have him executed. ·When they had carried out
everything that scripture foretells about him they
took him down from the tree and buried him
30   in a tomb. ·But God raised him from the dead,
31   and for many days he appeared to those who had
accompanied him from Galilee to Jerusalem: and
it is these same companions of his who are now
his witnesses before our people.

32   "We have come here to tell you the Good
News. It was to our ancestors that God made the
33   promise but ·it is to us, their children, that he has
fulfilled it, by raising Jesus from the dead. As
scripture says in the first psalm: You are my son:
34   today I have become your father. ·The fact that
God raised him from the dead, never to return
to corruption, is no more than what he had declared: To you I shall give the sure and holy things
35   promised to David. ·This is explained by another
text: You will not allow your holy one to expe-
36   rience corruption. ·Now when David in his own
time had served God's purposes he died; he was
buried with his ancestors and has certainly ex-
37   perienced corruption. ·The one whom God has
raised up, however, has not experienced corruption.

38   "My brothers, I want you to realize that it is
through him that forgiveness of your sins is proclaimed. Through him justification from all sins
39   which the Law of Moses was unable to justify ·is
offered to every believer.

40   "So be careful—or what the prophets say will
happen to you.

41   Cast your eyes around you, mockers;
        be amazed, and perish!

For I am doing something in your own days
that you would not believe if you were to be
told of it."

42   As they left they were asked to preach on the
43 same theme the following sabbath. ·When the
meeting broke up many Jews and devout converts joined Paul and Barnabas, and in their talks
with them Paul and Barnabas urged them to remain faithful to the grace God had given them.
44   The next sabbath almost the whole town assem-
45 bled to hear the word of God. ·When they saw the
crowds, the Jews, prompted by jealousy, used
blasphemies and contradicted everything Paul
46 said. ·Then Paul and Barnabas spoke out boldly.
"We had to proclaim the word of God to you first,
but since you have rejected it, since you do not
think yourselves worthy of eternal life, we must
47 turn to the pagans. ·For this is what the Lord commanded us to do when he said:

I have made you a light for the nations,
so that my salvation may reach the ends of the
earth."

48   It made the pagans very happy to hear this and
they thanked the Lord for his message; all who
were destined for eternal life became believers.
49 Thus the word of the Lord spread through the
whole countryside.
50   But the Jews worked upon some of the devout
women of the upper classes and the leading men
of the city and persuaded them to turn against
Paul and Barnabas and expel them from their ter-
51 ritory. ·So they shook the dust from their feet in
52 defiance and went off to Iconium; ·but the disciples were filled with joy and the Holy Spirit.

✠

In this section we encounter another major speech.
Readers would do well to take time to refresh their
memories on what was said about speeches in the com-

mentary on 2:14–41. Once that refresher course has been completed, we will explore (1) how Luke uses this speech to develop his story in Acts, and (2) how he uses it to preach to his community.

We will see how this speech functions by taking glances forward and backward in Acts. First, let's look ahead. In 14:3 we read: "Accordingly Paul and Barnabas stayed on for some time, preaching fearlessly for the Lord." In 14:25 Luke writes: "Then after proclaiming the word at Perga." Acts 18:11 reads: "So Paul stayed there [in Corinth] preaching the word of God among them for eighteen months." In these passages and many others in chapters 13–20 it is merely said that Paul preached; rarely are we given the content of that preaching. The section at hand is an exception and is Luke's paradigm of missionary preaching to Jews, devout converts (13:43), and God-fearers (13:17, 26). Since Luke has shown his readers through this idealized missionary sermon how Paul preaches to Jews, he has no need to go into further detail in subsequent chapters. It should be noticed that Paul's speech on the Areopagus (17:22–34) is the exemplar of his sermons to pagans (see 14:15–17 for a foreshadowing of that model sermon). Paul's words of encouragement to Christians in 14:22, 18:23, and 20:1–2 are climaxed in his sermon to Christian elders in 20:17–35. This forward look highlights one aspect of this section: it contains a model of missionary preaching to a Jewish audience.

Still looking forward in Acts, we come across two very important passages. One is 26:15–16: "And the Lord answered, 'I am Jesus, and you are persecuting me. But get up and stand on your feet, for I have appeared to you for this reason: to appoint you as my servant and as *witness* of this vision in which you have seen me, and of others in which I shall appear to you' "

(see also 22:15). Paul may not be an apostolic witness
(13:30–31; see the commentary on 1:15–26), but this
outstanding missionary to the gentiles is God's thir-
teenth witness. The other passage is 21:21: "They
[thousands of Jewish believers] have heard that you
instruct all Jews living among the pagans to break away
from Moses, authorizing them not to circumcise their
children or to follow the customary practices." This
passage echoes 13:38–39, 44–45; Paul's statements
about the Law of Moses will form the background for
chapters 21 through 26 of Acts.

If we look backward and compare this speech with
others in Acts, we note that its main parallels are to the
speeches of Peter. In the brief space available here we
sketch two parallels: the earthly ministry of Jesus, and
the witnesses to Jesus' resurrection:

> . . . about Jesus of Nazareth and how he began
> in Galilee, after *John had been preaching bap-
> tism.* [10:37]

> . . . Jesus, as Savior, whose coming was
> heralded by *John when he proclaimed a bap-
> tism* of repentance for the whole people of Is-
> rael. [13:24]

> *God raised him* to life and allowed him to be
> seen, not by the whole people but only by cer-
> tain *witnesses* God had chosen beforehand.
> Now we are those *witnesses*—we have eaten and
> drunk with him after his resurrection from the
> dead—and he has ordered us to proclaim this *to
> his people.* [10:40–42]

> But *God raised him* from the dead, and for
> many days he appeared to those who had ac-
> companied him from Galilee to Jerusalem: and

> it is these same companions of his who are now
> his *witnesses before our people*. [13:30–31]

These parallels intimate that Paul preaches the same
message which Peter (and the Twelve) preach. Paul's
message is not an inferior message, nor is it a message
which contradicts what the twelve apostles preached.

Let's continue our backward glance into the first volume of Luke's two-volume work and detect a further
parallel in Jesus' inaugural sermon at Nazareth (Lk
4:16–30; see *Invitation to Luke*, pp. 68–70). In both
there is a synagogue service with readings; the key
figure is invited to address the congregation. The Jews
first accept the preacher, and then many reject him.
Both sections refer to the mission to the pagans. Jesus'
sermon occurs at the commencement of his public ministry, Paul's at the beginning of his. Luke is purposely
comparing Paul to Jesus. Paul carried out the mission
to the pagans foretold in Jesus' first act of public ministry. The reader should be advised that Luke will continue this parallelism between Jesus and Paul. It was
predicted for both Jesus and Paul that they would journey to Jerusalem and suffer: "I am on my way to
Jerusalem, but have no idea what will happen to me
there, except that the Holy Spirit, in town after town,
has made it clear enough that imprisonment and persecution await me" (Ac 20:22–23).

What message does Luke preach to his community
via the sermon of this section? First, he assures them
that Paul is not a renegade, whose message and life had
little to do with the Twelve and Jesus (see the Introduction for more detail). Second, he supports their
faith that they stand in continuity with the history of
the people for whom God cared so lavishly (see the
references to "our/us" in 13:17, 31, 32, 33). Finally,
God has fulfilled his promise for Luke's generation of

Jewish and gentile Christians (see 13:23, 29, 32–33).
That promise is specifically fulfilled and evidenced in
Jesus' resurrection, which effects eternal life for believ-
ers (see 13:33, 46, 48).

This section unfolds Luke's presentation of the role
Paul has in the fulfillment of the promise the Risen
Jesus made in 1:8. Paul, like Peter, continues Jesus'
mission.

STUDY QUESTIONS: Why would the Jews be "prompted
by jealousy" (13:45)? Why is
there no mention of baptism or the
gift of the Spirit in this section (see
13:48–49)? Does the "we must
turn to the pagans" of 13:46 state
a missionary principle? If so, how
does one explain those passages in
which it is said that Paul does further missionary work in Jewish
synagogues (14:1; 17:1, 10, 17;
18:4, 19, 26; 19:8)?

PERSECUTION FURTHERS CHRISTIAN MISSION AND LIFE

¹ **14** At Iconium they went to the Jewish synagogue, as they had at Antioch, and they spoke so effectively that a great many Jews and Greeks became believers.

² Some of the Jews, however, refused to believe, and they poisoned the minds of the pagans against the brothers.

³ Accordingly Paul and Barnabas stayed on for some time, preaching fearlessly for the Lord; and the Lord supported all they said about his gift of grace, allowing signs and wonders to be performed by them.

⁴ The people in the city were divided, some supported the Jews, others the apostles, ·but eventually with the connivance of the authorities a move was made by pagans as well as Jews to make attacks on them and to stone them. ·When the apostles came to hear of this, they went off for safety to Lycaonia where, in the towns of Lystra and Derbe and in the surrounding country, ·they preached the Good News.

⁸ A man sat there who had never walked in his life, because his feet were crippled from birth; ⁹ and as he listened to Paul preaching, he managed to catch his eye. Seeing that the man had the faith to be cured, ·Paul said in a loud voice, "Get to your feet—stand up," and the cripple jumped up and began to walk.

¹¹ When the crowd saw what Paul had done they shouted in the language of Lycaonia, "These people are gods who have come down to us disguised as men." ·They addressed Barnabas as Zeus, and since Paul was the principal speaker they called

13 him Hermes. ·The priests of Zeus-outside-the-
Gate, proposing that all the people should offer
sacrifice with them, brought garlanded oxen to the
14 gates. ·When the apostles Barnabas and Paul heard
what was happening they tore their clothes, and
15 rushed into the crowd, shouting, ·"Friends, what
do you think you are doing? We are only human
beings like you. We have come with good news to
make you turn from these empty idols to the living
God who made heaven and earth and the sea and
16 all that these hold. ·In the past he allowed each na-
17 tion to go its own way; ·but even then he did not
leave you without evidence of himself in the good
things he does for you: he sends you rain from
heaven, he makes your crops grow when they
should, he gives you food and makes you happy."
18 Even this speech, however, was scarcely enough
to stop the crowd offering them sacrifice.
19 Then some Jews arrived from Antioch and
Iconium, and turned the people against the apostles. They stoned Paul and dragged him outside
20 the town, thinking he was dead. ·The disciples
came crowding around him but, as they did so, he
stood up and went back to the town. The next day
he and Barnabas went off to Derbe.
21 Having preached the Good News in that town
and made a considerable number of disciples,
they went back through Lystra and Iconium to
22 Antioch. ·They put fresh heart into the disciples,
encouraging them to persevere in the faith. "We
all have to experience many hardships," they said,
23 "before we enter the kingdom of God." ·In each
of these churches they appointed elders, and with
prayer and fasting they commended them to the
Lord in whom they had come to believe.
24 They passed through Pisidia and reached Pam-
25 phylia. ·Then after proclaiming the word at Perga
26 they went down to Attalia ·and from there sailed
for Antioch, where they had originally been commended to the grace of God for the work they
had now completed.
27 On their arrival they assembled the church and
gave an account of all that God had done with

them, and how he had opened the door of faith to
28 the pagans. ·They stayed there with the disciples
for some time.

✠

There are six points to be noticed in this account of
the continuation and completion of the missionary en-
deavors of Paul and Barnabas.

The first point is Luke's tendency to abbreviate.
Events which might have taken months to accomplish
are telescoped into the grandiose happenings of a single
day. Luke's presentation gives the impression of a missionary blitzkrieg, with Paul and Barnabas storming
through Asia Minor. If we look at the distances and
time involved, we may obtain a more sober impression
of what happened on this first missionary journey. The
distance between Perga and Antioch is one hundred
miles, and Antioch is 3,900 feet above sea level. Iconium is about eighty-five miles southeast of Antioch.
Lystra is twenty-three miles southwest of Iconium, and
Derbe is fifty-six miles southeast of Lystra. And the
main means of transportation was by foot! Some
scholars have estimated that it took Paul and Barnabas
three years (A.D. 46–49) to complete this first missionary journey. Luke's presentation might be compared to
talks I've heard from missionaries on furlough. In one
hour a missionary had to present the signal achieve-
ments and key events of three years. He condensed, ex-
aggerated, and used heavy doses of local color to entertain and edify us, all the while taking the risk that he
might give the impression that three years' work occurred overnight.

Secondly, in this section Luke continues a theme he
inaugurated in 13:13–52: Paul is equivalent to Peter
and the other apostles. "And the Lord supported all

they said about his gift of grace, allowing signs and
wonders to be performed by them" (14:3) is a clear
echo of what is said of the twelve apostles: "many signs
and wonders were worked among the people at the
hands of the apostles" (5:12). The equality between
Peter and Paul is not only shown by such general corre-
spondences; Paul produces the works of Jesus just as
Peter did by restoring a cripple from birth to health
(compare 14:8–10 with 3:1–10; see the commentaries
on 3:1–10 and 9:32–43).

The third point has "persecution" painted brightly
across it (14:5, 19–20, 22). Luke drastically abbrevi-
ates Paul's recovery to image him as the indomitable
missionary whose zeal overcomes such a trivial obstacle
as a mere stoning (14:19–20). Luke's message is one
of hope: from persecution comes growth.

The fourth point concerns the terms "apostles" and
"elders." The word "apostles" occurs in 14:4 and 14
(the JB introduces "apostles" also in verses 6 and 19,
but it does not appear there in the Greek), yet we know
from the commentary on 1:15–26 that Paul cannot be
an apostle because he has not been a witness of the
earthly life of Jesus. This inconsistency might be resolved by maintaining that Luke allows another meaning of "apostle"—envoy of the Antioch church—to remain in his sources. (The word "apostle" means,
literally, "one sent.") That this might be the meaning
of "apostle" here is indirectly confirmed by the fact
that this missionary venture of the Antioch church is
not subject to the apostles in Jerusalem. Paul and Barnabas return to Antioch, not Jerusalem, for confirmation of what God had wrought through their hands
(14:26–27). The missionaries Paul and Barnabas appoint elders (14:23; see 20:17). Luke apparently uses
a word from the Jewish wing of his church or its tradition to describe people in charge of the Jewish Chris-

tian communities founded by Paul. The Paul of the genuine letters does not employ the term "elder" (the word rendered "presiding elders" in Philippians 1:1 in The Jerusalem Bible is literally "bishops").

For the fifth point, turn your attention to 14:11–18. The brief polemic against idolatry (14:15–17) anticipates Paul's model and longer sermon to pagans in Athens (17:22–34). Although the missionaries may appear extraordinary because of their single-minded dedication and healing powers, they are not divine men worthy of worship (14:15, 18).

Finally, the successful mission of the Antioch church to Jews and gentiles was the result not of human enterprise but of God's will: "On their arrival they assembled the church and gave an account of *all that God had done with them,* and *how he had opened* the door of faith to the pagans" (14:27).

STUDY QUESTION: Why would missionaries like Paul and Barnabas continue their mission and preach "fearlessly for the Lord" (14:3) in the face of innumerable obstacles?

GENTILES DO NOT NEED CIRCUMCISION AND THE MOSAIC LAW TO BE SAVED

¹ 15 Then some men came down from Judaea and taught the brothers, "Unless you have yourselves circumcised in the tradition of Moses
² you cannot be saved." ·This led to disagreement, and after Paul and Barnabas had had a long argument with these men it was arranged that Paul and Barnabas and others of the church should go up to Jerusalem and discuss the problem with the apostles and elders.

³ All the members of the church saw them off, and as they passed through Phoenicia and Samaria they told how the pagans had been converted, and this news was received with the greatest satis-
⁴ faction by the brothers. ·When they arrived in Jerusalem they were welcomed by the church and by the apostles and elders, and gave an account of all that God had done with them.

⁵ But certain members of the Pharisees' party who had become believers objected, insisting that the pagans should be circumcised and instructed
⁶ to keep the Law of Moses. ·The apostles and elders
⁷ met to look into the matter, ·and after the discussion had gone on a long time, Peter stood up and addressed them.

"My brothers," he said, "you know perfectly well that in the early days God made his choice among you: the pagans were to learn the Good
⁸ News from me and so become believers. ·In fact God, who can read everyone's heart, showed his approval of them by giving the Holy Spirit to
⁹ them just as he had to us. ·God made no distinction between them and us, since he purified their
¹⁰ hearts by faith. ·It would only provoke God's

anger now, surely, if you imposed on the disciples
the very burden that neither we nor our ancestors
11 were strong enough to support? ·Remember, we
believe that we are saved in the same way as they
are: through the grace of the Lord Jesus."

12   This silenced the entire assembly, and they listened to Barnabas and Paul describing all the signs
and wonders God had worked through them
among the pagans.

13   When they had finished it was James who
spoke. "My brothers," he said, "listen to me.
14 Simeon has described how God first arranged to
enlist a people for his name out of the pagans.
15 This is entirely in harmony with the words of the
prophets, since the scriptures say:

16   After that I shall return
and rebuild the fallen House of David;
I shall rebuild it from its ruins
and restore it.
17   Then the rest of mankind,
all the pagans who are consecrated to my name,
will look for the Lord,
18   says the Lord who made this ·known so long
ago.

19   "I rule, then, that instead of making things more
20 difficult for pagans who turn to God, ·we send
them a letter telling them merely to abstain from
anything polluted by idols, from fornication, from
the meat of strangled animals and from blood.
21 For Moses has always had his preachers in every
town, and is read aloud in the synagogues every
sabbath."

22   Then the apostles and elders decided to choose
delegates to send to Antioch with Paul and Barnabas; the whole church concurred with this. They
chose Judas known as Barsabbas and Silas, both
23 leading men in the brotherhood, ·and gave them
this letter to take with them:

"The apostles and elders, your brothers, send
greetings to the brothers of pagan birth in An-
24 tioch, Syria and Cilicia. ·We hear that some of
our members have disturbed you with their de-

mands and have unsettled your minds. They acted

25 without any authority from us, ·and so we have
decided unanimously to elect delegates and to
send them to you with Barnabas and Paul, men

26 we highly respect ·who have dedicated their lives

27 to the name of our Lord Jesus Christ. ·Accord-
ingly we are sending you Judas and Silas, who will
confirm by word of mouth what we have written

28 in this letter. ·It has been decided by the Holy
Spirit and by ourselves not to saddle you with any

29 burden beyond these essentials: ·you are to abstain from food sacrificed to idols, from blood,
from the meat of strangled animals and from
fornication. Avoid these, and you will do what is
right. Farewell."

30   The party left and went down to Antioch, where
they summoned the whole community and deliv-

31 ered the letter. ·The community read it and were
delighted with the encouragement it gave them.

32 Judas and Silas, being themselves prophets, spoke
for a long time, encouraging and strengthening

33 the brothers. ·These two spent some time there,
and then the brothers wished them peace and they

35 went back to those who had sent them. ·Paul and
Barnabas, however, stayed on in Antioch, and
there with many others they taught and proclaimed the Good News, the word of the Lord.

✠

Many years ago a wise man scratched his balding
head, looked me straight in the eye, and then shared a
profound truth with me: "Son, there's no growth without pain." There was no bitterness in his voice, no cyn-
icism. His was the happy voice of experience. He had
shared a secret of a lifetime with me, and it didn't cost
me a penny. Since that time I have learned how true his
experience was. I have also learned that such lived experience bears a high price tag. In many ways this section is like the revelation I received from the wise man.

The truth of this section as expressed in its title, "Gentiles do not need circumcision and the Mosaic Law to be saved," can roll off our lips as smoothly and as effortlessly as a mountain stream. But costly effort stands behind the reality of that statement and is demanded of us if we are going to fathom the meaning of that simple title. We travel through this section in three stages: (1) the key place of this section in the story of Acts; (2) the historical problems generated by this section; (3) Luke's intention in this section.

The key place of this section in the story of Acts. Since chapter 10 Luke has been concerned with the conditions under which pagans can be saved. In this section he rounds off the treatment of that problem by introducing a radical viewpoint: "Unless you have yourselves circumcised in the tradition of Moses you cannot be saved" (15:1); "pagans should be circumcised and instructed to keep the Law of Moses" (15:5). Against these viewpoints Peter argues that circumcision is not necessary for salvation: "Remember, we believe that we are saved in the same way as they are: through the grace of the Lord Jesus" (15:11). James argues that the gentiles just have to observe the four Old Testament injunctions which were made for them: (1) do not eat anything polluted by idols (15:20, 29; see Lv 17:8–9); (2) abstain from marriage within certain bonds of consanguinity (15:20, 29; see Lv 18:6–18; the JB translation should have used "uncleanness" here rather than the too narrow term "fornication"); (3) abstain from the meat of strangled animals since this meat still has blood in it (15:20, 29; see Lv 17:13–14); (4) abstain from blood (15:20, 29; see Lv 17:10–12). When these authoritative solutions of Peter and James were communicated, the communities "were delighted with the encouragement [they] gave them" (see 15:31). In the story of Acts a critical

obstacle has been squarely faced, openly debated, and
happily overcome. Paul can continue the mission to the
gentiles—unhindered—and be the witness to "the ends
of the earth" (see 1:8).

The historical problems generated by this section.
Problems surface if we go over this section carefully
and if we compare it with passages in Paul's letters. A
white-glove treatment of this section reveals the dust
that Peter's speech in 15:7–11 and James's in 15:13–21
do not speak of the same issues and are even somewhat
contradictory. The Simeon in 15:14 appears to be Peter
until one realizes that Luke calls Peter Peter in 15:7
and Simon Peter in 10:5, 18, and 32. Nowhere else
does he call him Simeon. In an earlier version of this
account Simeon may well have been Simeon called
Niger (see 13:1). In 15:16–18 James's arguments are
dependent not on the Hebrew text of the prophet Amos
(Am 9:11–12) as one would expect of the Jewish
leader James but upon the variants introduced in the
Greek translation of those verses. Where does Silas, who
had returned to Jerusalem, join Paul for the latter's second missionary journey (contrast 15:33 with 15:40)?
Turning to the letters of Paul, we crash head-on with
Galatians 2:1–14, which does not mention the ruling
of James. If this ruling had been made in Paul's presence or communicated to him, he surely would have
made use of it in 1 Corinthians 8:13 and 10:14–30,
where the issue at stake was meat sacrificed to idols.
But he does not. How does one explain these historical
problems?

A reasonable solution to these problems would be
that in Acts 15 Luke combines two Jerusalem meet-
ings. In the first meeting, whose description ends with
15:12, Peter agrees with Paul and endorses the position of a Gentile mission without circumcision. This
meeting is also detailed by Paul in Galatians 2:1–10.

The second meeting occurred later and dealt with the problem of table fellowship between Jewish and gentile Christians. An example of the problems involved can be seen in Galatians 2:11–14. During that meeting James used his authority to resolve the problem of table fellowship by issuing the ruling found in 15:20 and 15:29. It seems that Paul was not present for this second meeting since Acts 21:25 says that Paul is first advised of James's ruling when he meets James in Jerusalem after his third missionary journey. Since Paul does not know of the ruling, it is easy to see why he does not enforce it in his communities, e.g., in Corinth. Acts 16:4 refers to the decision that circumcision is not necessary for salvation.

Luke's intention in this section. Struggling through the historical problems which mine this section has no doubt taught the reader that growth in knowledge is purchased at the cost of no little effort. Seen from another perspective, this section embodies truths which grew out of long and painful discussions and soul-searching on the part of Luke's communities. Luke's missionaries could preach the good news to pagans and announce to them that they did not have to be circumcised to be saved. These pagan converts lived in concord with their fellow Christians of Jewish origin because they observed the four commandments for gentiles found in the scriptures which were read during their weekly worship service (15:21). These solutions had cost Luke's readers much. And Luke reminds his communities that they must continue to pay the cost of living out these truths as these truths are assaulted by Jewish Christian missionaries who poach on Lukan mission territory and teach the salvific necessity of circumcision and the entire Mosaic Law (see 15:1 and 5). To compound matters, these folk malign Paul, a hero of the Lukan communities, and charge that Paul speaks against the Law (see the commentary on 21:25). Luke defends his missionary praxis and the praxis of his church by appealing to Peter's intervention (15:7-11) and to James's ruling (15:13-29). Who can gainsay the teaching of such Jewish Christian stalwarts as Peter and James? As a matter of fact, it is the law-abiding James, and not Paul, who has relaxed the burden of the Law for pagan converts.

STUDY QUESTIONS: There are many changes occurring in the church today. Are any of them as drastic as the conversion of gentiles without imposing circumcision or the Mosaic Law on them? How is it that a decision arrived at by James, the apostles, and elders, is called a decision of the Holy Spirit (15:28)?

THE BEGINNING OF PAUL'S SECOND MISSIONARY JOURNEY

36 On a later occasion Paul said to Barnabas, "Let us go back and visit all the towns where we preached the word of the Lord, so that we can see 37 how the brothers are doing." ·Barnabas suggested 38 taking John Mark, ·but Paul was not in favor of taking along the very man who had deserted them in Pamphylia and had refused to share in their work.

39 After a violent quarrel they parted company, and Barnabas sailed off with Mark to Cyprus. 40 Before Paul left, he chose Silas to accompany him and was commended by the brothers to the grace of God.

41 He traveled through Syria and Cilicia, consolidating the churches.

1 **16** From there he went to Derbe, and then on to Lystra. Here there was a disciple called Timothy, whose mother was a Jewess who had be- 2 come a believer; but his father was a Greek. ·The brothers at Lystra and Iconium spoke well of 3 Timothy, ·and Paul, who wanted to have him as a traveling companion, had him circumcised. This was on account of the Jews in the locality where everyone knew his father was a Greek.

4 As they visited one town after another, they passed on the decisions reached by the apostles and elders in Jerusalem, with instructions to respect them.

5 So the churches grew strong in the faith, as well as growing daily in numbers.

6 They traveled through Phrygia and the Galatian country, having been told by the Holy Spirit not to

⁷ preach the word in Asia. ·When they reached the frontier of Mysia they thought to cross it into Bithynia, but as the Spirit of Jesus would not al-
⁸ low them, ·they went through Mysia and came down to Troas.
⁹   One night Paul had a vision: a Macedonian appeared and appealed to him in these words,
¹⁰ "Come across to Macedonia and help us." ·Once he had seen this vision we lost no time in arranging a passage to Macedonia, convinced that God had called us to bring them the Good News.

✠

Some time ago I went to a hockey game. A power play formed at my end of the rink. The puck was shot from the right point and blocked in front of the goal. There was a scramble. I strained to see what was happening. All of a sudden the red light went on. A goal had been scored. And I had missed it. So much had happened so fast that I yearned to see the play again in slow motion on instant replay. This relatively brief section is like that quick play. So much is happening that we must move through the section in slow motion.

15:36–41 Paul wants to revisit the churches he and Barnabas founded (15:36). But the Spirit has other plans for him; Paul must embark on a new mission (see 16:6–10). With a slight blush on his cheeks Luke says that even such outstanding missionaries as Paul and Barnabas had their acrimonious differences of opinion and separated (15:39). Paul enlists Silas, a leading Jerusalem Christian (15:22; see also 15:27, 32), as his fellow missionary and thus maintains ties with the center of Christianity (15:40). Paul first journeys through Syria and Cilicia and strengthens the faith of communities he had not founded (15:41; see the commentaries on 13:1 to 14:28).

16:1–5 Timothy no doubt was a gem of a convert (16:1–3). From one point of view he was considered Jewish since his mother was Jewish. From another point of view he was considered illegitimate since he came from a mixed and therefore illegitimate marriage. Paul does not have Timothy circumcised so that he might be saved. Peter and Paul had resolved that problem earlier (15:7–11). He is circumcised so that he might function more effectively as a Jewish Christian missionary among his fellow Jewish Christian missionaries, who otherwise might be scandalized that a Jew who had been raised as a gentile graced their ranks. Luke floodlights Paul as one who is very well attuned to Jewish sensitivities. Paul delivers the decisions of the Jerusalem council to churches outside the pale of the original decrees (see 15:23). Paul is faithful to Jerusalem, its apostles and elders, and its traditions. Because of his fidelity his churches flourish (16:5).

16:6–10 Luke seems to have streamlined his account to focus on the importance of the new mission into Europe (see the commentary on 14:1–28). The missionary's bedfellows of a tired body, sleepless nights spent in discerning God's will, etc, are placed on the back burner to accent God's direction of Paul's mission.

STUDY QUESTION: Why is Luke so concerned to show that Paul's second missionary journey, which lasted from A.D. 49 to 52, was connected with Jerusalem and was directed by the Spirit of Jesus?

Acts 16:11–40
LESSONS GLEANED FROM THE MISSION AT PHILIPPI

11   Sailing from Troas we made a straight run for
12 Samothrace; the next day for Neapolis, ·and from
there for Philippi, a Roman colony and the principal city of that particular district of Macedonia.
13 After a few days in this city ·we went along the
river outside the gates as it was the sabbath and
this was a customary place for prayer. We sat
down and preached to the women who had come
14 to the meeting. ·One of these women was called
Lydia, a devout woman from the town of Thyatira
who was in the purple-dye trade. She listened to
us, and the Lord opened her heart to accept what
15 Paul was saying. ·After she and her household
had been baptized she sent us an invitation: "If
you really think me a true believer in the Lord,"
she said, "come and stay with us"; and she would
take no refusal.

16   One day as we were going to prayer, we met a
slave girl who was a soothsayer and made a lot
of money for her masters by telling fortunes.
17 This girl started following Paul and the rest of us
and shouting, "Here are the servants of the Most
High God; they have come to tell you how to be
18 saved!" ·She did this every day afterward until
Paul lost his temper one day and turned around
and said to the spirit, "I order you in the name of
Jesus Christ to leave that woman." The spirit went
out of her then and there.

19   When her masters saw that there was no hope
of making any more money out of her, they
seized Paul and Silas and dragged them to the law
20 courts in the market place ·where they charged
them before the magistrates and said, "These peo-

ple are causing a disturbance in our city. They are
21 Jews ·and are advocating practices which it is
unlawful for us as Romans to accept or follow."
22 The crowd joined in and showed its hostility to
them, so the magistrates had them stripped and
23 ordered them to be flogged. ·They were given
many lashes and then thrown into prison, and the
24 jailer was told to keep a close watch on them. ·So,
following his instructions, he threw them into the
inner prison and fastened their feet in the stocks.
25   Late that night Paul and Silas were praying and
singing God's praises, while the other prisoners
26 listened. ·Suddenly there was an earthquake that
shook the prison to its foundations. All the doors
flew open and the chains fell from all the prison-
27 ers. ·When the jailer woke and saw the doors wide
open he drew his sword and was about to commit
suicide, presuming that the prisoners had escaped.
28 But Paul shouted at the top of his voice, "Don't do
yourself any harm; we are all here."
29   The jailer called for lights, then rushed in,
threw himself trembling at the feet of Paul and
30 Silas, ·and escorted them out, saying, "Sirs, what
31 must I do to be saved?" ·They told him, "Become
a believer in the Lord Jesus, and you will be saved,
32 and your household too." ·Then they preached the
word of the Lord to him and to all his family.
33 Late as it was, he took them to wash their wounds,
and was baptized then and there with all his house-
34 hold. ·Afterward he took them home and gave
them a meal, and the whole family celebrated their
conversion to belief in God.
35   When it was daylight the magistrates sent the
36 officers with the order: "Release those men." ·The
jailer reported the message to Paul, "The magistrates have sent an order for your release; you can
37 go now and be on your way." ·"What!" Paul replied. "They flog Roman citizens in public and
without trial and throw us into prison, and then
think they can push us out on the quiet! Oh no!
They must come and escort us out themselves."
38   The officers reported this to the magistrates,
who were horrified to hear the men were Roman

39 citizens. ·They came and begged them to leave the
40 town. ·From the prison they went to Lydia's house
    where they saw all the brothers and gave them
    some encouragement; then they left.

☩

Before launching into the five missionary lessons this
section inculcates, let us pause briefly to examine the
"we" passages in Acts. This section includes one of
them, 16:10–17. The others are 20:5–15; 21:1–18;
and 27:1 to 28:16. Scholars are divided on the question of whether the "we" includes Luke, the author of
Acts. There is good reason to believe, however, that the
"we" passages contain some historically reliable material but do not prove that Luke was a traveling companion of Paul. In writing about the missionary travels
of Paul, Luke has on occasion adapted the literary
form of a sea voyage: The author is not present on the
voyage, but he uses the first person plural to add liveli-
ness to his narrative. This solution helps to account for
the anomaly that the person behind the "we" accompa-
nies Paul almost exclusively on sea voyages. Soon after
Paul touches land, the "we" style trails off.

The first lesson of this section is that Christianity has
success among the rich (see also 17:4, 12). Lydia, a
dealer in purple, is wealthy and "devout"—i.e., attached
to Judaism as a God-fearer (16:14). She and her
household are baptized (16:15). In order to appreciate
the significance of this conversion, we must expand our
notion of household beyond the norm provided by the
IRS. A recent author correctly observes: "In New Testament times the household was regarded as a basic political unity. In addition to members of the immedi-
ate family, slaves, freedmen, servants, laborers, and
sometimes business associates and tenants were included. . . . The closeness of the household unit

offered the security and sense of belonging not provided by larger political and social structures" (A. J. Malherbe, *Social Aspects of Early Christianity* [Baton Rouge: Louisiana State University Press, 1977], p. 69). A rich woman's house becomes the base for the Christian mission in Philippi (see 16:40). From the data available on whom a household comprised, it is not certain that the baptism of an entire household included baptism of infants.

Lesson two is almost buried in 16:15: "She sent us an invitation: 'If you really think me a true believer in the Lord,' she said, 'come and stay with us'; and she would take no refusal." Why does Lydia urge Paul and his companions to accept her hospitality? In the Judaism with which Lydia had been affiliated, a non-Jewish convert was on a lower social level than the "born" Jew. Hospitality extended and accepted is concrete proof that the "born" Christian in Luke's time is not superior to a recent convert like Lydia; social inequality is absent.

Lesson three is familiar to the reader from 8:4–25. The Jesus Paul preaches is superior to soothsaying spirits (16:18).

The fourth lesson revolves around the question of the relationship of Christianity to the Roman Empire. In 16:19–24 it seems that the Roman authorities punish Paul and Silas only because the actions and motives of these missionaries are misrepresented to them. Luke's view of Roman officialdom is generally positive —e.g., in 13:4–12 and 26:32. Luke has four reasons for this. First, he wants to teach his persecuted community the Roman Empire is reasonable and will correct its mistakes. Second, his persecuted community should champion its rights and not give in to the Roman authorities too readily (see 16:35–39). Third, Roman authorities are not gigantic ogres who are programmed to destroy Christians engaged in missionary work. Finally, pagan converts-to-be have nothing to fear from the Roman authorities if they become Christians.

The final lesson of this section issues from 16:25–34. Luke, a great storyteller, uses folktale elements to depict God's intervention in the lives of Paul and Silas (see the commentaries on 4:1–22 and 4:23–31 for more details). That intervention is in answer to prayer (16:25). The suffering of Paul and Silas is not in vain, for it leads to the conversion of the jailer and his household (16:32–33). Paul and Silas—and missionaries like them—continue Jesus' life. The pattern of Jesus' victory through suffering is reproduced in his missionaries.

STUDY QUESTION: To what extent are the missionary lessons of this section relevant for contemporary mission?

Acts 17:1–15
LUKE'S STYLIZATION AND UPDATING OF PAUL'S MISSIONARY ACTIVITIES

¹ 17 Passing through Amphipolis and Apollonia, they eventually reached Thessalonika, ² where there was a Jewish synagogue. ·Paul as usual introduced himself and for three consecutive sabbaths developed the arguments from scripture ³ for them, ·explaining and proving how it was ordained that the Christ should suffer and rise from the dead. "And the Christ," he said, "is this Jesus ⁴ who I am proclaiming to you." ·Some of them were convinced and joined Paul and Silas, and so did a great many God-fearing people and Greeks, as well as a number of rich women.

⁵ The Jews, full of resentment, enlisted the help of a gang from the market place, stirred up a crowd, and soon had the whole city in an uproar. They made for Jason's house, hoping to find them there and drag them off to the People's Assembly; ⁶ however, they only found Jason and some of the brothers, and these they dragged before the city council, shouting, "The people who have been turning the whole world upside down have come ⁷ here now; ·they have been staying at Jason's. They have broken every one of Caesar's edicts by claim- ⁸ ing that there is another emperor, Jesus." ·This accusation alarmed the citizens and the city coun- ⁹ cilors ·and they made Jason and the rest give security before setting them free.

¹⁰ When it was dark the brothers immediately sent Paul and Silas away to Beroea, where they visited the Jewish synagogue as soon as they arrived. ¹¹ Here the Jews were more open-minded than those in Thessalonika, and they welcomed the word very readily; every day they studied the scriptures

¹² to check whether it was true. ·Many Jews became
      believers, and so did many Greek women from the
      upper classes and a number of the men.
¹³   When the Jews of Thessalonika heard that the
      word of God was being preached by Paul in
      Beroea as well, they went there to make trouble
¹⁴ and stir up the people. ·So the brothers arranged
      for Paul to go immediately as far as the coast,
¹⁵ leaving Silas and Timothy behind. ·Paul's escort
      took him as far as Athens, and went back with in-
      structions for Silas and Timothy to rejoin Paul as
      soon as they could.

☩

We noticed in the commentary on 14:1–28 that
Luke stylizes his account of Paul's missions. This section provides us with further examples of Luke's styli-
zation. First, Luke is silent on how Paul spent the time
from sabbath to sabbath (17:2). In a major speech at
Miletus Paul says: "I have never asked anyone for
money or clothes; you know for yourselves that the
work I did earned enough to meet my needs and those
of my companions" (20:33–34). Paul was a tentmaker
(see 18:3). Second, "Paul as usual" went to the Jewish
synagogue (17:2) is shorthand for his missionary practice (see 13:5, 14; 14:1; 16:13; 17:10, 17; 18:4, 19;
19:8; 28:17, 23). Third, that persecution and plots
from Jews terminate a missionary endeavor is also
shorthand (see 14:5–6, 19; 17:5, 13–14; 18:12–13;
19:33; 20:3, 19; 21:11; 23:12; harassment from pagans is noticed in 16:19–20 and 19:23–43). This last
element of abbreviation calls for further comment.

During these days when many of us take very
seriously the challenge to eliminate our sexist language,
we are updating our hymns. "Rise Up, O Men of God"
becomes "Rise Up, O People of God." Caught in the
vortex of this change, we can appreciate the vast implications of the substitution of one word for another.

Something similar is reflected in Luke's mention that the "Jews" persecute Paul. From Paul's first letter to the Thessalonians it seems that he and the Thessalonian Christians were persecuted by non-Jews: "For you, my brothers, have been like the churches of God in Christ Jesus which are in Judaea, in suffering the same treatment from *your own countrymen* as they have suffered from the Jews" (1 Th 2:14; see also 3:1–4). In Acts 17:5, 13–14 the persecution stems from Jews. It may be that Luke has "updated" his version of what happened in Thessalonika to meet a situation of his own day where some of his Christian missionaries were being persecuted by Jews. For them he presents the example of a fearless Paul. Paul's preaching to the Jews will ultimately lead to his death, yet to his dying days he continues to fulfill God's will and preach to them. Luke's missionaries should do the same (see the commentary on 28:17–31 for more detail). Some Jews will be converted (see 13:43; 14:1; 17:4, 12; 18:8; 19:8–9; 28:24).

Two additional points in Luke's updating. "Full of resentment" (17:5) is literally "full of jealousy" (see also 13:45 and 5:17). The jealousy was prompted by the realization that the financially well-heeled God-fearers were being lured away by the Christian missionaries. The accusation against Paul in 17:7 ("They have broken every one of Caesar's edicts by claiming that there is another emperor, Jesus") may echo similar charges leveled against Luke's missionaries (see also 16:21; 18:13; 19:37; 21:28).

STUDY QUESTION: Jason has to put money on the line for harboring Paul (17:9). Why would a convert of a few weeks suffer the loss of material goods to be faithful to God's call?

Acts 17:16–34
A PARADIGM OF MISSIONARY
PREACHING TO GENTILES

16   Paul waited for them in Athens and there his whole soul was revolted at the sight of a city given
17 over to idolatry. ·In the synagogue he held debates with the Jews and the God-fearing, but in the market place he had debates every day with any-
18 one who would face him. ·Even a few Epicurean and Stoic philosophers argued with him. Some said, "Does this parrot know what he's talking about?" And, because he was preaching about Jesus and the resurrection, others said, "He sounds like a propagandist for some outlandish gods."
19   They invited him to accompany them to the Council of the Areopagus, where they said to him, "How much of this new teaching you were speak-
20 ing about are we allowed to know? ·Some of the things you said seemed startling to us and we
21 would like to find out what they mean." ·The one amusement the Athenians and the foreigners living there seem to have, apart from discussing the latest ideas, is listening to lectures about them.
22   So Paul stood before the whole Council of the Areopagus and made this speech:

"Men of Athens, I have seen for myself how extremely scrupulous you are in all religious mat-
23 ters, ·because I noticed, as I strolled around admiring your sacred monuments, that you had an altar inscribed: To An Unknown God. Well, the God whom I proclaim is in fact the one whom you already worship without knowing it.
24   "Since the God who made the world and everything in it is himself Lord of heaven and earth, he does not make his home in shrines made by

²⁵ human hands. ·Nor is he dependent on anything that human hands can do for him, since he can never be in need of anything; on the contrary, it is he who gives everything—including life and ²⁶ breath—to everyone. ·From one single stock he not only created the whole human race so that they could occupy the entire earth, but he decreed how long each nation should flourish and what ²⁷ the boundaries of its territory should be. ·And he did this so that all nations might seek the deity and, by feeling their way toward him, succeed in finding him. Yet in fact he is not far from any ²⁸ of us, ·since it is in him that we live, and move, and exist, as indeed some of your own writers have said:

'We are all his children.'

²⁹ "Since we are the children of God, we have no excuse for thinking that the deity looks like anything in gold, silver or stone that has been carved and designed by a man.

³⁰ "God overlooked that sort of thing when men were ignorant, but now he is telling everyone ³¹ everywhere that they must repent, ·because he has fixed a day when the whole world will be judged, and judged in righteousness, and he has appointed a man to be the judge. And God has publicly proved this by raising this man from the dead."

³² At this mention of rising from the dead, some of them burst out laughing; others said, "We ³³ would like to hear you talk about this again." ·After ³⁴ that Paul left them, ·but there were some who attached themselves to him and became believers, among them Dionysius the Areopagite and a woman called Damaris, and others besides.

✠

Athens symbolized Greek culture and sophistication. Its mention would trigger thoughts and emotions in Luke's readers similar to those which the mention of

Harvard evokes for us. Small wonder that Luke did not
have Paul deliver this speech to the pagans at Lystra, where the opportunity to do so first knocked
(14:15-17). That would have made about as much an
impression on Luke's readers as a major address delivered at Boondock University would on us. Luke has
set the stage well for his message. We follow his story
in three acts: (1) Luke's purpose; (2) how Luke
achieves his purpose; (3) the dual portraiture of Paul.

Luke's purpose. In 13:13-52 Luke had used Paul to
present a model of preaching to Jews. In this section
he gives his missionary communities a paradigm of
preaching to the gentiles. In both instances Paul's
preaching is successful (see 13:43, 48; 17:34). If we
combine Paul's sermon to Jews in 13:13-53 with this
one to pagans, we detect another aspect of Luke's purpose. He wants to show his readers what "the whole of
God's purpose" is for all of humankind, Jew and gentile (see 20:27).

How Luke achieves his purpose. Luke achieves his
purpose by literary and theological means. On the literary level Luke engages his reader's interest by decking
Paul out in some of the literary clothes worn by that
great Greek hero and model Socrates. Like Socrates,
Paul debates in the market place (17:17) and is re-
viled as a spokesman for "some outlandish gods"
(17:18). Also on the literary level Luke uses words
with universal connotations to highlight the fact that
God's purpose embraces everything: "everything"
(17:24); "everything . . . everyone" (17:25); "whole
. . . entire" (17:26); "everyone everywhere" (17:30);
"whole" (17:31).

On the theological level Luke makes use of both Old
Testament and popular Stoic thought to achieve his
purpose. For example, Acts 17:24 is a paraphrase of
Isaiah 42:5: "Thus says God, Yahweh, he who created

the heavens and spread them out, who gave shape to
the earth and what comes from it, who gave breath to
its people and life to the creatures that move in it"
(also compare Ac 17:29 with Is 44:9–20). Stoic-
sounding are "he is not far from any of us" (17:27)
and "in him we live, and move, and exist" (17:28).
Missionary preaching to the gentiles should combine
Old Testament revelation, Greek religious and philosophical inspirations, and Christian revelation. On this
last point verses 30–31 are key. God has excused both
Jew and gentile of their previous behavior because they
acted in ignorance of his will (compare 17:36 with
3:17–19; 7:60; and 13:27). God revealed himself and
his will by raising Jesus from the dead (17:31). Because of this revelation the pagans became acquainted
with the Unknown God whom they have been worship-
ing (17:23). They are to repent, for in God's purpose
there is a judgment (17:31).

The dual portraiture of Paul. As we noted in the
commentary on 9:20–31, Acts and the letters of Paul
often display different portraits of Paul. Some scholars
are quick to contrast the optimistic view of pagans in
this section with the pessimistic view of them found in
Romans 1:19–21: "For what can be known about God
is perfectly plain to them since God himself has made it
plain. Ever since God created the world his everlasting
power and deity—however invisible—have been there
for the mind to see in the things he has made. That is
why such people are *without excuse:* they knew God
and yet refused to honor him as God or to thank him;
instead, they made nonsense out of logic and their
empty minds were darkened." This contrast can be
toned down by attending to the different purposes of
each author. Luke's purpose is to model, in Paul's
name, missionary preaching to the gentiles. Paul's purpose is to achieve his goal of proving that "both Jew

and pagan sinned and forfeited God's glory" (Rm 3:23). It should be noted that Paul, en route to proving his point that the Jews have sinned, makes positive statements about the gentile quest for God and salvation (see Rm 2).

In sum, Luke unfurls for his missionaries the sterling example of Paul's preaching to the gentiles. They should imitate him. At the same time they should prudently learn that the mere mention of "rising from the dead" will be a stumbling block (17:32). Yet that aspect of the message cannot be abandoned since it is God's revelation (17:31) and *the* connection between Christianity and God's revelation in Judaism (see 24:14–16).

STUDY QUESTIONS: To what extent can Christian preaching incorporate philosophical elements into its proclamation and still be considered Christian? Why is Jesus' resurrection so cardinal for Luke?

¹ ² **18** After this Paul left Athens and went to Corinth, ·where he met a Jew called Aquila whose family came from Pontus. He and his wife Priscilla had recently left Italy because an edict of Claudius had expelled all the Jews from Rome. ³ Paul went to visit them, ·and when he found they were tentmakers, of the same trade as himself, he lodged with them, and they worked together. ⁴ Every sabbath he used to hold debates in the synagogues, trying to convert Jews as well as Greeks.

⁵ After Silas and Timothy had arrived from Macedonia, Paul devoted all his time to preaching, declaring to the Jews that Jesus was the ⁶ Christ. ·When they turned against him and started to insult him, he took his cloak and shook it out in front of them, saying, "Your blood be on your own heads; from now on I can go to the pagans ⁷ with a clear conscience." ·Then he left the synagogue and moved to the house next door that belonged to a worshiper of God called Justus. ⁸ Crispus, president of the synagogue, and his whole household, all became believers in the Lord. A great many Corinthians who had heard him be- ⁹ came believers and were baptized. ·One night the Lord spoke to Paul in a vision, "Do not be afraid to speak out, nor allow yourself to be silenced: ¹⁰ I am with you. I have so many people on my side in this city that no one will even attempt to hurt ¹¹ you." ·So Paul stayed there preaching the word of God among them for eighteen months.

¹² But while Gallio was proconsul of Achaia, the Jews made a concerted attack on Paul and ¹³ brought him before the tribunal. ·"We accuse this man," they said, "of persuading people to wor-

14 ship God in a way that breaks the Law." ·Before
   Paul could open his mouth, Gallio said to the
   Jews, "Listen, you Jews. If this were a misde-
   meanor or a crime, I would not hesitate to at-
15 tend to you; ·but if it is only quibbles about words
   and names, and about your own Law, then you
   must deal with it yourselves—I have no intention
   of making legal decisions about things like that."
16
17 Then he sent them out of the court, ·and at once
   they all turned on Sosthenes, the synagogue president, and beat him in front of the courthouse.
   Gallio refused to take any notice at all.

☩

In this section three familiar themes rub shoulders
with one another. After a few Jews are converted and
the majority of the Jews reject Paul, Paul preaches to
the gentiles (18:5–8; see the commentary on 17:1–15
for more detail). God is faithful to the promises he
makes (see 18:12–17, where the promise of 18:9–10
is fulfilled). The Roman authorities are benevolent toward the Christians (18:1–17; see the commentary on
16:11–40 for more detail).

These three themes brush up against one another because Luke has drawn in the walls of eighteen months
(18:11) to form the tiny space of a few weeks (on the
Lukan tendency to abbreviate the events of Paul's mission, see the commentaries on 14:1–28 and 17:1–15).
Instead of illustrating Paul's mission in Corinth with
three hundred slides, Luke selects the three most telling
ones.

In highlighting his major themes and in putting Paul
in the forefront, Luke is not able to give adequate
attention to the key figures Aquila and Priscilla
(18:1–3). From this description of them we could not
even be sure that they were Christians. But we can
infer from Paul's references to them in his letters that

these two well-off Christians were very influential in his missionary effort. Luke's data might be profitably supplemented by what Paul says in Romans 16:3-5: "My greetings to Prisca and Aquila, my fellow workers in Christ Jesus, who risked death to save my life: I am not the only one to owe them a debt of gratitude, all the churches among the pagans do as well. My greetings also to the church that meets at their house."

The peculiar gesture of rejection in 18:16—"He took his cloak and shook it out in front of them"—is paralleled in Nehemiah 5:13: "Then I shook out the lap of my gown with the words, 'May God do this, and shake out of his house and property any man who does not keep this promise; may he be shaken out like this and left empty.' "

STUDY QUESTION: Why would Paul dedicate a full year and a half of his short missionary career to evangelizing the cosmopolitan capital city of the Roman province of Achaia?

Acts 18:18–28
PAUL, MISSIONARY PAR EXCELLENCE

18 After staying on for some time, Paul took leave of the brothers and sailed for Syria, accompanied by Priscilla and Aquila. At Cenchreae he had his hair cut off, because of a vow he had made.

19 When they reached Ephesus, he left them, but first he went alone to the synagogue to debate with 20 the Jews. ·They asked him to stay longer but he 21 declined, ·though when he left he said, "I will come back another time, God willing." Then he sailed from Ephesus.

22 He landed at Caesarea, and went up to greet the 23 church. Then he came down to Antioch ·where he spent a short time before continuing his journey through the Galatian country and then through Phrygia, encouraging all the followers.

24 An Alexandrian Jew named Apollos now arrived in Ephesus. He was an eloquent man, with a sound knowledge of the scriptures, and yet, 25 though he had been given instruction in the Way of the Lord and preached with great spiritual earnestness and was accurate in all the details he taught about Jesus, he had only experienced 26 the baptism of John. ·When Priscilla and Aquila heard him speak boldly in the synagogue, they took an interest in him and gave him further instruction about the Way.

27 When Apollos thought of crossing over to Achaia, the brothers encouraged him and wrote asking the disciples to welcome him. When he arrived there he was able by God's grace to help 28 the believers considerably ·by the energetic way he refuted the Jews in public and demonstrated from the scriptures that Jesus was the Christ.

✠

Approaching the meaning of this section is like trying to pet a porcupine. Caution is the order of the day.

There are five quills in this section which can cause
us some problems. First, what is the nature of the vow
which Paul makes (18:18)? Second, Paul says good-
bye to Priscilla and Aquila and presumably to Ephesus.
But then Luke has Paul open up a "one-night" cam-
paign in the synagogue of Ephesus (18:19–21). Why?
Third, Paul went up to Jerusalem (18:22; "go up" is
a standard expression for going to Jerusalem). Why
does Luke deem it important to narrate that Paul
greeted the church in Jerusalem? Fourth, 18:23 is
the beginning of the so-called Third Missionary Journey (A.D. 54–57; see 18:23 to 21:17). But why does
Luke give the impression that Paul returns to Antioch
merely for a change of clothing before dashing off again
for the missions? Finally, was Apollos' teaching accurate or not (18:25)? If it was, why did he need further
instruction (18:26)?

We can avoid these quills and become acquainted
with the meaning of this section if we query Luke's
purpose in dedicating the entire last portion of Acts to
Paul. Paul is not a renegade Jew, as some Jewish and
Jewish Christian opponents of Luke's community con-
tend. He is such an exemplar of Jewish piety that he
even takes private vows (see the commentary on
22:1–29 for more detail on Luke's presentation of
Paul's fidelity to Jewish law and ritual). Paul is the
missionary par excellence for Luke. Priscilla, Aquila,
and Apollos may have a more important role in found-
ing the churches in various cities, but they are overshad-
owed by Luke's Paul. They are like people who warm
up the audience for the headline preacher. But even the

great Paul is no free-lance missionary; he has ties with Jerusalem and the mother church there.

STUDY QUESTION: Chapters 3 and 4 of 1 Corinthians underline the greatness of the missionary Apollos. Why does Luke present him as needful of further instruction from Paul's colleagues Priscilla and Aquila?

Acts 19:1–7
RATIFICATION OF THE
EPHESIAN MISSION

¹ 19 While Apollos was in Corinth, Paul made
his way overland as far as Ephesus, where
² he found a number of disciples. ·When he asked,
"Did you receive the Holy Spirit when you became believers?" they answered, "No, we were
never even told there was such a thing as a Holy
³ Spirit." ·"Then how were you baptized?" he asked.
⁴ "With John's baptism," they replied. ·"John's baptism," said Paul, "was a baptism of repentance;
but he insisted that the people should believe in
the one who was to come after him—in other
⁵ words Jesus." ·When they heard this, they were
⁶ baptized in the name of the Lord Jesus, ·and the
moment Paul had laid hands on them the Holy
Spirit came down on them, and they began to
⁷ speak with tongues and to prophesy. ·There were
about twelve of these men.

⌖

Some of the problems which we encountered in
18:18–28 are still with us in this section. Three problems call for special attention. First, how can the twelve
be "disciples" (19:1) and "believers" (19:2) and still
not have received the Holy Spirit? Second, why does
Luke dismiss these twelve disciples from the stage and
develop 19:8–10 as if Paul were the first missionary
to make disciples in Ephesus? Third, why is 19:1–7
here? Since Luke makes a fresh beginning in 19:8–10,

it seems that he could have positioned 19:1–7 almost anywhere in his story of Paul's missionary activity.

Three observations will protect us from the problems generated by this section. First, Ephesus is the most important base for Paul's mission. He spends at least two years here (19:10). Luke does not depict Paul as a Johnny-come-lately here. But someone else has evangelized Ephesus before Paul. As the Holy Spirit ratified the groundbreaking mission to Samaria through the hands of Peter and John, so the Spirit ratifies the prior mission to Ephesus through Paul's hands (see the commentary on 8:4–25 for more detail on the parallels between the mission to Samaria and the mission to Ephesus). Second, the twelve prophesy (19:6). It seems that Paul's imposition of hands incorporates these twelve people into his mission band (note that the passages which describe the external manifestations of the Spirit do not mention the missionary gift of prophesy; contrast 2:4, 6; 8:17; and 10:46). Third, because of the number and richness of traditions available to him (see the commentary on 19:8–41), Luke does not develop this tradition about the missionary work performed in Ephesus before Paul arrived on the scene.

STUDY QUESTION: Some commentators have interpreted this difficult section as Luke's attempt to incorporate a fringe group—the disciples of John the Baptist—into the "mainstream" church. Are there any indications in Acts that Luke could not "tolerate" pluralism or diversity in the church? See the commentary on 6:1–7.

THE WORD OF THE LORD SUCCEEDS

⁸   He began by going to the synagogue, where he spoke out boldly and argued persuasively about the kingdom of God. He did this for three months,
⁹ till the attitude of some of the congregation hardened into unbelief. As soon as they began attacking the Way in front of the others, he broke with them and took his disciples apart to hold daily dis-
¹⁰ cussions in the lecture room of Tyrannus. ·This went on for two years, with the result that people from all over Asia, both Jews and Greeks, were able to hear the word of the Lord.

¹¹   So remarkable were the miracles worked by
¹² God at Paul's hands ·that handkerchiefs or aprons which had touched him were taken to the sick, and they were cured of their illnesses, and the evil spirits came out of them.

¹³   But some itinerant Jewish exorcists tried pronouncing the name of the Lord Jesus over people who were possessed by evil spirits; they used to say, "I command you by the Jesus whose spokes-
¹⁴ man is Paul." ·Among those who did this were
¹⁵ seven sons of Sceva, a Jewish chief priest. ·The evil spirit replied, "Jesus I recognize, and I know who
¹⁶ Paul is, but who are you?" ·and the man with the evil spirit hurled himself at them and overpowered first one and then another, and handled them so violently that they fled from that house naked and
¹⁷ badly mauled. ·Everybody in Ephesus, both Jews and Greeks, heard about this episode; they were all greatly impressed, and the name of the Lord Jesus came to be held in great honor.

¹⁸   Some believers, too, came forward to admit in
¹⁹ detail how they had used spells ·and a number of them who had practiced magic collected their

books and made a bonfire of them in public. The
value of these was calculated to be fifty thousand
silver pieces.

20 In this impressive way the word of the Lord
spread more and more widely and successfully.

21 When all this was over Paul made up his mind
to go back to Jerusalem through Macedonia and
Achaia. "After I have been there," he said, "I
22 must go on to see Rome as well." ·So he sent two
of his helpers, Timothy and Erastus, ahead of him
to Macedonia, while he remained for a time in
Asia.

23 It was during this time that a rather serious disturbance broke out in connection with the Way.
24 A silversmith called Demetrius, who employed a
large number of craftsmen making silver shrines
25 of Diana, ·called a general meeting of his own
men with others in the same trade. "As you men
know," he said, "it is on this industry that we de-
26 pend for our prosperity. ·Now you must have
seen and heard how, not just in Ephesus but
nearly everywhere in Asia, this man Paul has persuaded and converted a great number of people
with his argument that gods made by hand are
27 not gods at all. ·This threatens not only to dis-
credit our trade, but also to reduce the sanctuary
of the great goddess Diana to unimportance. It
could end up by taking away all the prestige of a
goddess venerated all over Asia, yes, and every-
28 where in the civilized world." ·This speech roused
them to fury, and they started to shout, "Great is
29 Diana of the Ephesians!" ·The whole town was in
an uproar and the mob rushed to the theater drag-
ging along two of Paul's Macedonian traveling
30 companions, Gaius and Aristarchus. ·Paul wanted
to make an appeal to the people, but the disciples
31 refused to let him; ·in fact, some of the Asiarchs,
who were friends of his, sent messages imploring
him not to take the risk of going into the theater.

32 By now everybody was shouting different things
till the assembly itself had no idea what was going
on; most of them did not even know why they had
33 been summoned. ·The Jews pushed Alexander to

the front, and when some of the crowd shouted
encouragement he raised his hand for silence in
the hope of being able to explain things to the
34 people. ·When they realized he was a Jew, they all
started shouting in unison, "Great is Diana of the
Ephesians!" and they kept this up for two hours.
35 When the town clerk eventually succeeded in
calming the crowd, he said, "Citizens of Ephesus!
Is there anybody alive who does not know that
the city of the Ephesians is the guardian of the
temple of great Diana and of her statue that fell
36 from heaven? ·Nobody can contradict this and
there is no need for you to get excited or do any-
37 thing rash. ·These men you have brought here are
not guilty of any sacrilege or blasphemy against
38 our goddess. ·If Demetrius and the craftsmen he
has with him want to complain about anyone,
there are the assizes and the proconsuls; let them
39 take the case to court. ·And if you want to ask
any more questions you must raise them in the
40 regular assembly. ·We could easily be charged
with rioting for today's happenings: there was no
ground for it all, and we can give no reason for
41 this gathering." ·When he had finished this speech
he dismissed the assembly.

✠

Blazoned across the sky of this section are the words
"In this impressive way the word of the Lord spread
more and more widely and *successfully*" (19:20).
Luke paints Paul in awe-inspiring colors; he is at the
peak of his missionary powers. All competition melts
before him. Although there is distant murmuring from
the Jews (19:9, 33–34), Christianity through Paul has
overcome all forces: Jewish rejection, magic, and
pagan cults. After this section Luke will begin to whisper into his readers' ears that Paul will be martyred.
Although that whisper will become a stage whisper,
Luke never dedicates a scene to that event of which all

his readers are painfully aware—Paul's martyrdom.
Paul's remarkable triumph in Ephesus is just one side
of the Christian missionary coin of suffering and exaltation.

In this section Luke features the huge success of
Paul's last missionary enterprise and thus sculptures a
towering statue of Paul, the great missionary. His purpose is to summon his missionary community to draw
inspiration from Paul. Luke has accentuated seven
points for their meditation. First, the missionary church
should be encouraged in their mission to the Jews.
Some will be converted (19:9). Second, they should
continue to erect missionary bases in the urban centers.
From there the Word will spread successfully to the
outlying populations (19:10). Third, the Christian missionary does not travel alone. Both men and women
missionaries are endowed with certain powers
(19:11–12; see the commentary on 4:36 to 5:11).
Fourth, Christian missionaries should have no fear of
Jewish or Hellenistic or Christian magic. The name of
Jesus is more powerful than all of them combined
(19:13–19; see the commentaries on 8:4–25 and
13:1–12). Fifth, the Christian missionary effort is
directed by God. Paul's "I *must* go on" (19:31) is
Lukan terminology for "it is *God's will*." Sixth, the
Christian mission has established and will continue
to establish significant beachheads on pagan shores
(19:26). Finally, Roman religious leaders like the
Asiarchs, who were cultic officials of the Roman religion, and Roman civil officials like the town clerk
will be shrewd enough to perceive that opposition to
Christianity often stems from economic self-interest
(19:25–27, 31, 35–41). Christian missionaries are encouraged by the realization that the highly regarded
and wealthy Asiarchs judge that Christianity is not dangerous to the Roman Empire. Shouting will not win

over the town clerk, who was the executive officer of the city.

Luke's missionary community can draw strength from Paul and the example of his Ephesian mission. The Christian mission will succeed.

STUDY QUESTION: The Christian mission at Ephesus succeeded against religious, magical, and political forces. Are any of these same general forces operative against Christian missionary work today?

Acts 20:1–16
PAUL'S FAREWELL GIFT
TO HIS COMMUNITIES

1 **20** When the disturbance was over, Paul sent for the disciples and, after speaking words of encouragement to them, said good-by and set 2 out for Macedonia. ·On his way through those areas he said many words of encouragement to 3 them and then made his way into Greece, ·where he spent three months. He was leaving by ship for Syria when a plot organized against him by the Jews made him decide to go back by way of 4 Macedonia. ·He was accompanied by Sopater, son of Pyrrhus, who came from Beroea; Aristarchus and Secundus who came from Thessalonika; Gaius from Doberus, and Timothy, as well as Tychicus and Trophimus who were from 5 Asia. ·They all went on to Troas where they 6 waited for us. ·We ourselves left Philippi by ship after the days of Unleavened Bread and met them five days later at Troas, where we stopped for a week.

7 On the first day of the week we met to break bread. Paul was due to leave the next day, and he preached a sermon that went on till the middle 8 of the night. ·A number of lamps were lit in the 9 upstairs room where we were assembled, ·and as Paul went on and on, a young man called Eutychus who was sitting on the window sill grew drowsy and was overcome by sleep and fell to the ground three floors below. He was picked up 10 dead. ·Paul went down and stooped to clasp the boy to him. "There is no need to worry," he said, 11 "there is still life in him." ·Then he went back upstairs where he broke bread and ate and car- 12 ried on talking till he left at daybreak. ·They took

the boy away alive, and were greatly encouraged.
¹³   We were now to go on ahead by sea, so we set sail for Assos, where we were to take Paul on board; this was what he had arranged, for he
¹⁴ wanted to go by road. ·When he rejoined us at Assos we took him aboard and went on to Mity-
¹⁵ lene. ·The next day we sailed from there and arrived opposite Chios. The second day we touched at Samos and, after stopping at Trogyllium, made
¹⁶ Miletus the next day. ·Paul had decided to pass wide of Ephesus so as to avoid spending time in Asia, since he was anxious to be in Jerusalem, if possible, for the day of Pentecost.

✠

This section is constructed out of two small and two large points.

The two small points are: (1) that Paul leaves Ephesus in full control and does not have to sneak out of the back door because of the silversmiths' "riot" (20:1); (2) Paul is a pious Jew who wants to celebrate the feast of Pentecost in Jerusalem (21:16; see the commentary on 18:18–28).

The two large points. First, Luke gives the impression that the seven men who accompany Paul are mere traveling companions (20:4). To center all attention on the significance of Paul's final journey to Jerusalem in imitation of Jesus (see the commentary on 21:1–14), Luke does not mention that Paul's companions guard the Jerusalem collection which Paul had gathered in the gentile churches (see the mere hint of the collection in Ac 24:17; contrast Rm 15:25–29). Second, another "we" passage begins at 20:5 and will run to 21:18. By itself this observation is not a major point; what are major are the two interruptions in this "we" passage—20:17–38 and 20:7–12. Paul's "farewell speech" in 20:17–38 is complemented by his "farewell act" in 20:7–12. In some respects this miracle story is similar to that of 9:36–43. But "breaking of bread" (20:7, 11), a Lukan modification of a traditional miracle story, makes this story unique. This is the first time since 2:42 that Luke has explicitly mentioned "breaking of bread" (see 16:34: a meal after baptism). Paul's "farewell act" for his missionary churches is the gift of the Eucharist. Expressed in other terms, Luke's modifications in 20:7 and 11 convey a powerful message: Luke's communities can imitate the community at Troas by having no need to worry (20:10) and by being greatly encouraged (20:12) since at the breaking of bread/Eucharist the same Lord is present who at Troas gave life to the boy through Paul (see the commentary on 27:35).

STUDY QUESTION: Why would the breaking of bread be such a source of encouragement to Luke's missionary communities?

Acts 20:17–38
THE LEGACY OF THE
MISSIONARY-PASTOR PAUL

17 From Miletus he sent for the elders of the
18 church of Ephesus. ·When they arrived he addressed these words to them:

"You know what my way of life has been ever
since the first day I set foot among you in Asia,
19 how I have served the Lord in all humility, with
all the sorrows and trials that came to me through
20 the plots of the Jews. ·I have not hesitated to do
anything that would be helpful to you; I have
preached to you, and instructed you both in public
21 and in your homes, ·urging both Jews and Greeks
to turn to God and to believe in our Lord Jesus.

22 "And now you see me a prisoner already in
spirit; I am on my way to Jerusalem, but have no
23 idea what will happen to me there, ·except that the
Holy Spirit, in town after town, has made it clear
enough that imprisonment and persecution await
24 me. ·But life to me is not a thing to waste words
on, provided that when I finish my race I have carried out the mission the Lord Jesus gave me—and
that was to bear witness to the Good News of
God's grace.

25 "I now feel sure that none of you among whom
I have gone about proclaiming the kingdom will
26 ever see my face again. ·And so here and now I
swear that my conscience is clear as far as all of
27 you are concerned, ·for I have without faltering
put before you the whole of God's purpose.

28 "Be on your guard for yourselves and for all the
flock of which the Holy Spirit has made you the
overseers, to feed the Church of God which he
29 bought with his own blood. ·I know quite well that
when I have gone fierce wolves will invade you

30 and will have no mercy on the flock. ·Even from
your own ranks there will be men coming forward
with a travesty of the truth on their lips to induce
31 the disciples to follow them. ·So be on your guard,
remembering how night and day for three years
I never failed to keep you right, shedding tears
32 over each one of you. ·And now I commend you to
God, and to the word of his grace that has power
to build you up and to give you your inheritance
among all the sanctified.

33   "I have never asked anyone for money or
34 clothes; ·you know for yourselves that the work I
did earned enough to meet my needs and those of
35 my companions. ·I did this to show you that this
is how we must exert ourselves to support the
weak, remembering the words of the Lord Jesus,
who himself said, 'There is more happiness in giving than in receiving.' "

36   When he had finished speaking he knelt down
37 with them all and prayed. ·By now they were all
in tears; they put their arms around Paul's neck
38 and kissed him; ·what saddened them most was his
saying they would never see his face again. Then
they escorted him to the ship.

✠

Paul, the model missionary, is on his way to martyrdom (see 20:24–25, 38). In this farewell speech—
the only speech Paul addresses exclusively to Christians
—he sums up his vast missionary and pastoral experience in a few memorable verses. These verses embody
Paul's legacy for Luke's missionary communities.

In order to capture the full import of Paul's farewell
speech, we should first filter our imaginations. In this
passage the "elders" (20:17) should not be imagined
as resident pastors who do not engage in missionary
work. Paul's speech is meant for missionaries, who like
Paul can spend three years (20:31) in one church as
pastor before moving on to evangelize other peoples.

Paul's speech overflows with meaning and rewards frequent meditation. We single out five points for our meditation. First, in 20:18–21 Paul's example in the face of opposition receives top billing. As a missionary and as a local pastor Paul experienced plots from the Jews. Yet these plots did not deter him from preaching to both Jew and gentile.

Second, Paul makes it emphatically clear that, despite the persecution he had to endure, he carried out "the mission the Lord gave" him (20:24). He declared "the whole of God's purpose" for both Jew and gentile (20:27; see the commentaries on 13:13–52 and 17:16–34).

Third, Paul warns the missionary-pastors of Ephesus that outside missionaries are going to swoop down on their missionary territory like fierce wolves. Some of their fellow missionary-pastors will turn the truth sour (20:28–32). The "fierce wolves" (20:29) are false prophets (see Mt 7:15: "Beware of false prophets who come to you disguised as sheep but underneath are ravenous wolves"). They may be Jewish or Jewish-Christian missionaries who will argue that the message of Paul, the founder of their church, did not contain "the whole purpose of God" (20:27; see the Introduction for more detail).

Fourth, the faithful missionary-pastors will be able to detect false missionaries and prophets by their life style and care for the weak (20:33–35). The example of Paul provides them with a benchmark against which to judge their conduct and that of others. A Christian writing contemporaneous with Acts helps us imagine the situation about which Luke warns. "Let every Apostle who comes to you be received as the Lord, but let him not stay more than one day, or if need be a second as well; but if he stay three days, he is a false prophet. And when an Apostle goes forth let him accept nothing but bread till he reach his night's lodging; but if he ask for money, he is a false prophet. . . . But whosoever shall say in a spirit 'Give me money, or something else,' you shall not listen to him; but if he tell you to give on behalf of others in want, let none judge him" (*The Didache,* 11.3–6, 13, Loeb translation).

Fifth, missionary-pastors are to imitate Paul's preaching to Jew and gentile and to preserve the traditional content of the Christian message, which is a rampart against "fierce wolves" and inside agitators. That traditional content is the backbone on which this farewell speech is built; it includes the following points:

—Repentance and faith: "to turn to God and to believe in our Lord Jesus" (20:21).

—Grace: "the Good News of God's grace" (20:24); "the word of his grace that has power to build you up and to give you your inheritance among all the sanctified" (20:32).

—God's kingdom: "I have gone about proclaiming the kingdom" (20:25). See Luke 8:1, where Jesus' missionary activity is described in the same words.

—Jesus' death: "to feed the Church of God which he bought with his own blood" (20:28). The church is God's covenant community obtained by Jesus' blood of the covenant shed on the cross (see Ex 24:8).

Paul departs. The elders and Luke's missionary communities are sad. But Paul has not left them empty-handed. His parting gift is the legacy of this speech.

STUDY QUESTION: The great missionary and founder of communities has departed. An era has ended. Is Paul's legacy sufficient to sustain Luke's communities and those of us who have followed after Paul?

¹ 21 When we had at last torn ourselves away from them and put to sea, we set a straight course and arrived at Cos; the next day we reached Rhodes, and from there went on to Pa-² tara. ·Here we found a ship bound for Phoenicia, ³ so we went on board and sailed in her. ·After sighting Cyprus and leaving it to port, we sailed to Syria and put in at Tyre, since the ship was to ⁴ unload her cargo there. ·We sought out the disciples and stayed there a week. Speaking in the Spirit, they kept telling Paul not to go on to Jeru-⁵ salem, ·but when our time was up we set off. Together with the women and children they all escorted us on our way till we were out of the town. When we reached the beach, we knelt down ⁶ and prayed; ·then, after saying good-by to each other, we went aboard and they returned home.

⁷ The end of our voyage from Tyre came when we landed at Ptolemais, where we greeted the ⁸ brothers and stayed one day with them. ·The next day we left and came to Caesarea. Here we called on Philip the evangelist, one of the Seven, and ⁹ stayed with him. ·He had four virgin daughters ¹⁰ who were prophets. ·When we had been there several days a prophet called Agabus arrived from ¹¹ Judaea ·to see us. He took Paul's girdle, and tied up his own feet and hands, and said, "This is what the Holy Spirit says, 'The man this girdle belongs to will be bound like this by the Jews in Jerusalem, ¹² and handed over to the pagans.' " ·When we heard this, we and everybody there implored Paul not to ¹³ go on to Jerusalem. ·To this he replied, "What are you trying to do—weaken my resolution by your tears? For my part, I am ready not only to be tied up but even to die in Jerusalem for the name of

14 the Lord Jesus." ·And so, as he would not be persuaded, we gave up the attempt, saying, "The
   Lord's will be done."

✠

In a recent conversation, a friend mentioned something almost in passing that triggered a chain reaction
in my memory; memories seemed to tumble from nowhere and link together in the train of one major idea.
Careful pondering of this section might occasion a similar chain reaction in your memory. The major idea in
this section is suffering—that of Jesus and that of Paul.
We can identify the individual cars in the train of this
idea by tracing the way this section alludes to other
Lukan passages.

Like Jesus, Paul resolutely goes to Jerusalem. Acts
21:11-13 finds clear echoes in Luke 9:51: "Now as
the time drew near for him to be taken up to heaven,
he resolutely took the road for Jerusalem" and in Luke
18:32: "For he will be handed over to the pagans."
Paul's "I am ready not only to be tied up but even to
die in Jerusalem for the name of the Lord Jesus"
(21:13) echoes Peter's boast to Jesus at the Last Supper: "I would be ready to go to prison with you, and to
death" (Lk 22:33). Unlike Peter, Paul will be faithful
to Jesus. Paul's resolution "to die in Jerusalem for the
name of the Lord Jesus" (21:13) is in fulfillment of
God's will for him: "I myself will show him how much
he himself must suffer for my name" (Ac 9:17). "The
Lord's will be done" (21:14) echoes Jesus' firm prayer
in the Garden of Olives: "Father, if you are willing,
take this cup away from me. Nevertheless, let your will
be done, not mine" (Lk 22:42).

From this brief comparison of texts it becomes clear
that the great missionary Paul retraces Jesus' steps,

journeys to Jerusalem, and will relive Jesus' experience of martyrdom (see also the commentaries on 13:13–52 and 19:8–41). But why has Luke taken such pains to parallel the last days of Paul's missionary career with those of Jesus? An answer is to be found in the observation that in 20:17–38 Luke had presented Paul as the model missionary. But upon whom does Paul model his life as a missionary? The answer is: upon Jesus, the prototypical missionary. But Jesus was martyred. Just as Jesus, the prime missionary, was not rejected by God but was vindicated in his resurrection and ascension, so too Paul, although martyred, will be vindicated by the missionary communities which Jesus' Spirit has founded through him. Put another way, just as martyrdom was not God's final word to Jesus, so too it is not God's final word to Paul and those missionaries who follow in his footsteps. Like Jesus and through him, Paul will triumph through suffering.

Luke does not conclude Acts with an account of Paul's martyrdom. He focuses on the outcome of Paul's suffering, not on the suffering itself. From that suffering comes missionary growth.

STUDY QUESTION: Luke's communities are tempted to withdraw from missionary work because of persecution and setbacks. Does Luke's portrait of Paul challenge and encourage them in their temptation?

PAUL UNDER ATTACK

15 After this we packed and went on up to Jeru-
16 salem. ·Some of the disciples from Caesarea accompanied us and took us to the house of a Cypriot with whom we were to lodge; he was called
Mnason and had been one of the earliest disciples.
17 On our arrival in Jerusalem the brothers gave
18 us a very warm welcome. ·The next day Paul went
with us to visit James, and all the elders were pres-
19 ent. ·After greeting them he gave a detailed account of all that God had done among the pagans
20 through his ministry. ·They gave glory to God
when they heard this. "But you see, brother," they
said, "how thousands of Jews have now become
believers, all of them staunch upholders of the
21 Law, and ·they have heard that you instruct all
Jews living among the pagans to break away from
Moses, authorizing them not to circumcise their
children or to follow the customary practices.
22 What is to be done? Inevitably there will be a
meeting of the whole body, since they are bound
23 to hear that you have come. ·So do as we suggest.
We have four men here who are under a vow;
24 take these men along and be purified with them
and pay all the expenses connected with the
shaving of their heads. This will let everyone
know there is no truth in the reports they have
heard about you and that you still regularly ob-
25 serve the Law. ·The pagans who have become believers, as we wrote when we told them our decisions, must abstain from things sacrificed to idols,
from blood, from the meat of strangled animals
and from fornication."
26 So the next day Paul took the men along and
was purified with them, and he visited the Temple

to give notice of the time when the period of puri-
fication would be over and the offering would
have to be presented on behalf of each of them.

27 The seven days were nearly over when some
Jews from Asia caught sight of him in the Temple
28 and stirred up the crowd and seized him, ·shout-
ing, "Men of Israel, help! This is the man who
preaches to everyone everywhere against our people, against the Law and against this place. Now
he has profaned this Holy Place by bringing
29 Greeks into the Temple." ·They had, in fact, previously seen Trophimus the Ephesian in the city
with him, and thought that Paul had brought him
into the Temple.

30 This roused the whole city; people came running from all sides; they seized Paul and dragged
him out of the Temple, and the gates were closed
31 behind them. ·They would have killed him if a
report had not reached the tribune of the cohort
32 that there was rioting all over Jerusalem. ·He immediately called out soldiers and centurions, and
charged down on the crowd, who stopped beating
Paul when they saw the tribune and the soldiers.
33 When the tribune came up he arrested Paul, had
him bound with two chains and inquired who he
34 was and what he had done. ·People in the crowd
called out different things, and since the noise
made it impossible for him to get any positive information, the tribune ordered Paul to be taken
35 into the fortress. ·When Paul reached the steps, the
crowd became so violent that he had to be carried
36 by the soldiers; ·and indeed the whole mob was
after them, shouting, "Kill him!"

37 Just as Paul was being taken into the fortress,
he asked the tribune if he could have a word with
him. The tribune said, "You speak Greek, then?
38 So you are not the Egyptian who started the recent revolt and led those four thousand cutthroats
39 out into the desert?" ·"I?" said Paul. "I am a Jew
and a citizen of the well-known city of Tarsus in
Cilicia. Please give me permission to speak to the
40 people." ·The man gave his consent and Paul,
standing at the top of the steps, gestured to the

people with his hand. When all was quiet again he
spoke to them in Hebrew.

✠

This section might be compared to the first act of a
six-act play. The play runs from chapter 21 to 26 and
bears the title "Paul and the Jewish Heritage." Some
characters and themes appear in this first act never to
return: James and the elders; the Jewish Christians.
Some characters and themes in this first act will appear
time and time again: Paul, the Jews, and the Roman
authorities.

First, let's look at the characters and themes that
cross the stage in this first act and then disappear forever. "James and all the elders" (21:18)—the authorities among the Jewish Christians—give their stamp of
approval on Paul's mission to the pagans (21:20) and
remind Paul and the readers of the few regulations required of the pagans (21:25). These authorities also
approve of Paul's observance of the Jewish Law, but
counsel him to defuse the suspicions of the Jewish
Christians (21:22–24). These Jewish Christians also
have a small walk-on part in the first act (21:20–21).
Their accusations will be picked up by the Jews from
Asia (21:28). One theme is conspicuous by its absence
from this first act: Paul's collection for the saints. For
the Paul of the letters, this collection was a sign of solidarity between the gentile Christians and the Jewish
Christians (see Rm 15:25–27). Perhaps Luke is silent
about the collection (but see 24:17 and the commentary on 11:19–30) because in his situation anything
connected with the name of Paul was suspect of
conflicting interpretations. Luke has enough work for
three hands in trying to clear Paul's reputation without

tackling a theme which would overly complicate the plot of his six-act play.

Secondly, spotlights single out the three main characters of this play: Paul, the Jews, the Roman authorities. In this first act *Paul* is depicted as a pious, law-abiding Jew (21:26). He will not step out of this character for the rest of the play (see 23:6; 24:11–21; 26:6–8). As Paul will state so dramatically in the last act: "I followed the strictest party in our religion and lived as a Pharisee. And now it is for my hope in the promise made by God to our ancestors that I am on trial, the promise that our twelve tribes, constant in worship night and day, hope to attain. For that hope, Sire, I am actually put on trial by Jews! Why does it seem incredible to you that God should raise the dead?" (26:5–8). This is a strange way for Paul to defend himself against the charges which the Jews level at him in 21:28: "This is the man who preaches to everyone everywhere against our people, against the Law and against this place. Now he has profaned this Holy Place by bringing Greeks into the Temple."

By making this observation about the strangeness of Paul's defense, we have directed *the Jews* to the center of the stage in act one and have anticipated what will develop in the remaining five acts. See 24:5–6 and 25:8 for passages very similar to 21:28. See 22:21–22 and 26:20–21, where it seems that the accusation made against Paul by the Jews is that he preaches to the pagans. As if Luke has not laid the basis for a sufficiently complex plot in this first act, he introduces a third main character in 21:37–40. *The Roman* tribune implicitly acknowledges the fact that Paul is not an insurrectionist in the tradition of the Egyptian leader of cutthroats. This theme of the innocence of Paul and the Christian mission will sound time and again in this play (see 23:39; 25:18–19; 25:24; 26:32). It crescendoes in 26:32: "This man is doing nothing that deserves death or imprisonment."

In this play, "Paul and the Jewish Heritage," Luke defends his missionary hero Paul from the accusations of Jews and Jewish Christians. In doing so, he also writes defense speeches for his own community as it endures similar charges from Jews and Jewish Christians.

STUDY QUESTIONS: As predicted, Paul is bound in Jerusalem by the pagans (see 21:11 and 33). Why would Luke devote six chapters to the story of an accused criminal? Why would Christians want to read about the lengthy trial of the great missionary Paul?

Acts 22:1–29
PAUL'S JEWISH BACKGROUND

¹ ² **22** "My brothers, my fathers, listen to what I have to say to you in my defense." ·When they realized he was speaking in Hebrew, the ³ silence was even greater than before. ·"I am a Jew," Paul said, "and was born at Tarsus in Cilicia. I was brought up here in this city. I studied under Gamaliel and was taught the exact observance of the Law of our ancestors. In fact, I was as full of duty toward God as you are today. ⁴ I even persecuted this Way to the death, and sent ⁵ women as well as men to prison in chains ·as the high priest and the whole council of elders can testify, since they even sent me with letters to their brothers in Damascus. When I set off it was with the intention of bringing prisoners back from there to Jerusalem for punishment.

⁶ "I was on that journey and nearly at Damascus when about midday a bright light from heaven ⁷ suddenly shone around me. ·I fell to the ground and heard a voice saying, 'Saul, Saul, why are you ⁸ persecuting me?' ·I answered: Who are you, Lord? and he said to me, 'I am Jesus the Nazarene ⁹ and you are persecuting me.' ·The people with me saw the light but did not hear his voice as he spoke ¹⁰ to me. ·I said: What am I to do, Lord? The Lord answered, 'Stand up and go into Damascus, and there you will be told what you have been ap- ¹¹ pointed to do.' ·The light had been so dazzling that I was blind and my companions had to take me by the hand; and so I came to Damascus.

¹² "Someone called Ananias, a devout follower of the Law and highly thought of by all the Jews ¹³ living there, ·came to see me; he stood beside me and said, 'Brother Saul, receive your sight.' In-

stantly my sight came back and I was able to see

14 him. ·Then he said, 'The God of our ancestors has
chosen you to know his will, to see the Just One

15 and hear his own voice speaking, ·because you are
to be his witness before all mankind, testifying to

16 what you have seen and heard. ·And now why
delay? It is time you were baptized and had your
sins washed away while invoking his name.'

17 "Once, after I had got back to Jerusalem, when
I was praying in the Temple, I fell into a trance

18 and then I saw him. 'Hurry,' he said, 'leave Jerusalem at once; they will not accept the testimony

19 you are giving about me.' ·Lord, I answered, it
is because they know that I used to go from
synagogue to synagogue, imprisoning and flogging

20 those who believed in you; ·and that when the
blood of your witness Stephen was being shed,
I was standing by in full agreement with his mur-

21 derers, and minding their clothes. ·Then he said
to me, 'Go! I am sending you out to the pagans
far away.' "

22 So far they had listened to him, but at these
words they began to shout, "Rid the earth of the

23 man! He is not fit to live!" ·They were yelling,
waving their cloaks and throwing dust into the

24 air, ·and so the tribune had him brought into the
fortress and ordered him to be examined under
the lash, to find out the reason for the outcry

25 against him. ·But when they had strapped him
down Paul said to the centurion on duty, "Is it
legal for you to flog a man who is a Roman citi-

26 zen and has not been brought to trial?" ·When he
heard this the centurion went and told the tribune;
"Do you realize what you are doing?" he said.

27 "This man is a Roman citizen." ·So the tribune
came and asked him, "Tell me, are you a Roman

28 citizen?" "I am," Paul said. ·The tribune replied,
"It cost me a large sum to acquire this citizen-

29 ship." "But I was born to it," said Paul. ·Then
those who were about to examine him hurriedly
withdrew, and the tribune himself was alarmed
when he realized that he had put a Roman citizen
in chains.

✠

This second act of "Paul and the Jewish Heritage" is rife with historical implausibilities and literary problems.

It strains credibility that: (1) Paul, badly beaten by the riotous crowd, would have the strength to address a large assembly; (2) the Roman authority would allow a rabble-rouser like Paul to address the crowd; (3) the crowd, livid with religious anger, would quiet down to listen to the person whose life they demanded (see 21:40 to 22:2). The literary problems are: (1) Does Paul's defense really address the accusations of the Jews (21:28)? (2) Why do details about Paul's call in this section differ from comparable ones in the call narratives of 9:1–19 and 26:12–18 (see the commentaries on those sections)? (3) Why does Paul's speech terminate with 22:21?

We may be able to explain these historical implausibilities and literary problems by inquiring into Luke's purpose in this second act. If we continue our image of a play, we realize that Luke, like the author of a play, is granted a certain license in the area of what might or might not be plausible. What is all-important is the point the author intends to make. And Luke's point is to underline the Jewishness of Paul and the Christian mission. This emphasis, made in various ways, forms an eloquent defense against the charges of 21:28 and shows that Paul and his churches stand in solid continuity with the Jewish heritage. Note the following salient points in Paul's defense:

—"My brothers, my fathers" (22:1).
—"I am a Jew" (22:3).
—"I . . . was taught the exact observance of the Law of our ancestors" (22:3).

—Ananias, conveyer of God's will to Paul, is "a devout follower of the Law and highly thought of by all the Jews" (22:12).

—"The God of our ancestors has chosen you" (22:14).

—Like a pious Jew, Paul prays in the Temple. In the center of Jewish religion Paul is instructed by God to preach to the pagans (22:17, 21).

Thus, the evidence of Paul's life is a strong voice in his defense against the charges of 21:28. Moreover, Paul's mission to the pagans is willed by God and consequently should not be seen as an attack on the privileged status of the Jewish people, or on the Law or on the Temple (21:28). In subsequent chapters Luke will marshal additional arguments to demonstrate Christianity's and Paul's ties with the Jewish heritage.

Luke's purpose is not fully mastered by these observations, though. In 22:17–21, Luke introduces a mystery into the play. The mystery is why Jews do not accept Paul's testimony. One would think that God's transformation of Paul, the zealous persecutor, would stir Jews to accept Paul's testimony (22:19–20). Yet the Jerusalem Jews do not (22:17), and God sends Paul to the pagans. Luke does not give further insight into this mystery in chapters 22–26. The mystery will thunder in the concluding verses of Acts (see the commentary on 28:17–31).

STUDY QUESTION: Does Paul present a convincing defense against the charges of 21:28?

Acts 22:30 to 23:35

CHRISTIANITY IS IN THE BEST TRADITION OF JUDAISM

³⁰ The next day, since he wanted to know what precise charge the Jews were bringing, he freed Paul and gave orders for a meeting of the chief priests and the entire Sanhedrin; then he brought Paul down and stood him in front of them.

¹ **23** Paul looked steadily at the Sanhedrin and began to speak, "My brothers, to this day I have conducted myself before God with a per-² fectly clear conscience." ·At this the high priest Ananias ordered his attendants to strike him on ³ the mouth. ·Then Paul said to him, "God will surely strike you, you whitewashed wall! How can you sit there to judge me according to the Law, and then break the Law by ordering a man ⁴ to strike me?" ·The attendants said, "It is God's ⁵ high priest you are insulting!" ·Paul answered, "Brothers, I did not realize it was the high priest, for scripture says: You must not curse a ruler of your people."

⁶ Now Paul was well aware that one section was made up of Sadducees and the other of Pharisees, so he called out in the Sanhedrin, "Brothers, I am a Pharisee and the son of Pharisees. It is for our hope in the resurrection of the dead that I am on ⁷ trial." ·As soon as he said this a dispute broke out between the Pharisees and Sadducees, and the as-⁸ sembly was split between the two parties. ·For the Sadducees say there is neither resurrection, nor angel, nor spirit, while the Pharisees accept all ⁹ three. ·The shouting grew louder, and some of the scribes from the Pharisees' party stood up and protested strongly, "We find nothing wrong with

this man. Suppose a spirit has spoken to him, or
10 an angel?" ·Feeling was running high, and the tribune, afraid that they would tear Paul to pieces,
ordered his troops to go down and haul him out
and bring him into the fortress.

11   Next night, the Lord appeared to him and said,
"Courage! You have borne witness for me in Jerusalem, now you must do the same in Rome."

12   When it was day, the Jews held a secret meeting at which they made a vow not to eat or drink
13 until they had killed Paul. ·There were more than
14 forty who took part in this conspiracy, ·and they
went to the chief priests and elders, and told
them, "We have made a solemn vow to let noth-
15 ing pass our lips until we have killed Paul. ·Now
it is up to you and the Sanhedrin together to apply
to the tribune to bring him down to you, as though
you meant to examine his case more closely; we,
on our side, are prepared to dispose of him before
he reaches you."

16   But the son of Paul's sister heard of the ambush
they were laying and made his way into the for-
17 tress and told Paul, ·who called one of the centurions and said, "Take this young man to the trib-
18 une; he has something to tell him." ·So the man
took him to the tribune, and reported, "The prisoner Paul summoned me and requested me to
bring this young man to you; he has something to
19 tell you." ·Then the tribune took him by the hand
and drew him aside and asked, "What is it you
20 have to tell me?" ·He replied, "The Jews have
made a plan to ask you to take Paul down to the
Sanhedrin tomorrow, as though they meant to in-
21 quire more closely into his case. ·Do not let them
persuade you. There are more than forty of them
lying in wait for him, and they have vowed not to
eat or drink until they have got rid of him. They
are ready now and only waiting for your order to
22 be given." ·The tribune let the young man go with
this caution, "Tell no one that you have given me
this information."

23   Then he summoned two of the centurions and
said, "Get two hundred soldiers ready to leave for

Caesarea by the third hour of the night with sev-
24 enty cavalry and two hundred auxiliaries; ·provide
horses for Paul, and deliver him unharmed to Fe-
25 lix the governor." ·He also wrote a letter in these
26 terms: ·"Claudius Lysias to his Excellency the gov-
27 ernor Felix, greetings. ·This man had been seized
by the Jews and would have been murdered by
them but I came on the scene with my troops and
got him away, having discovered that he was a
28 Roman citizen. ·Wanting to find out what charge
they were making against him, I brought him be-
29 fore their Sanhedrin. ·I found that the accusation
concerned disputed points of their Law, but that
there was no charge deserving death or imprison-
30 ment. ·My information is that there is a conspiracy
against the man, so I hasten to send him to you,
and have notified his accusers that they must state
their case against him in your presence."
31   The soldiers carried out their orders; they
took Paul and escorted him by night to Antipatris.
32 Next day they left the mounted escort to go on
33 with him and returned to the fortress. ·On arriv-
ing at Caesarea the escort delivered the letter to
34 the governor and handed Paul over to him. ·The
governor read the letter and asked him what province he came from. Learning that he was from
35 Cilicia he said, ·"I will hear your case as soon as
your accusers are here too." Then he ordered him
to be held in Herod's praetorium.

✠

With this section we are caught up in the drama of
the third act of "Paul and the Jewish Heritage." In this
act Luke devotes considerable attention to the development of the character of "the Jews." We comment on
the performances of the Romans, the Jews, and Paul
seriatim.

The Romans. The tribune, Claudius Lysias, continues to protect Paul from actual and potential Jewish attacks on his person (23:10, 23–25; see 22:25–29).

The tribune respects Paul's Roman citizenship (23:27; see 22:25–29), and writes: "I found that the accusation concerned disputed points of their Law, but that there was no charge deserving death or imprisonment" (23:29). Luke is using the way the Roman tribune treated Paul as a means of encouraging those Christians who were being harassed and accused before Roman officials (see the commentary on 16:11–40).

The Jews. Luke's portrayal of the Jews is complex and two-sided. First, a careful scrutiny of 23:1–10 indicates that this subsection is Lukan theology and not really Paul's apology. Since the members of the Sanhedrin were not present for the riot of 21:27–36, they didn't know the issues involved in the trial. Moreover, the tribune did not have authority to assemble the Sanhedrin. Finally, Paul does not answer the charges of 21:28, but pursues the question of the resurrection. Acts 23:1–10 is Luke's theological reflection on the situation in his community after the destruction of Jerusalem and its Temple (A.D. 70). The Sadducees and high priests are out of power. The Pharisees are in control of Judaism and are suspicious of Christianity. Luke presents Paul as explaining that both he and his Christian mission have intimate ties with Pharisaic beliefs. The Pharisees seem persuaded by this line of theological reasoning. Second, there are other Jews who plan to kill Paul and approach the chief priests and elders with their scheme (23:12–21). Presumably, the Jewish authorities acquiesce to their plot. Does Luke introduce the "more than forty" Jews here as dramatic "misdirection," whereby his audience is misdirected to expect them to return later in the play whereas they do not? Or does he introduce them here to create a contrast: some Jews will acknowledge that Paul, the Christian missionary, stands in valid continuity with the

Pharisaic Jewish heritage while others want his memory erased from the face of the earth?

Paul. True to character, Paul is the pious Jew—obedient to the Law (23:1), a Pharisee (23:6). As we have seen, his one-sentence apology is Lukan theology (23:6; see 24:21). While it does not answer the accusations of 21:28, it does help to show that Paul's life and Christianity flow from Pharisaic hope in a messiah and Pharisaic belief in the resurrection of the dead. Jesus, raised by God, is the Messiah; maybe his spirit addressed Paul outside the gates of Damascus (23:9).

Obviously, Luke's purpose in this section is not to plumb the depths of Paul's Christology or theology of the resurrection. He makes a simple and important point. Reflection on Paul's Pharisaic background can lead to the conviction that Christian belief is in the best tradition of Judaism.

STUDY QUESTION: Luke argues on the basis of what Judaism and Christianity have in common. How much value would this approach have in Jewish-Christian dialogues?

ROMAN POWER AND PAUL'S INNOCENCE

¹ **24** Five days later the high priest Ananias came down with some of the elders and an advocate named Tertullus, and they laid informa- ² tion against Paul before the governor. ·Paul was called, and Tertullus opened for the prosecution, "Your Excellency, Felix, the unbroken peace we enjoy and the reforms this nation owes to your ³ foresight ·are matters we accept, always and ev- ⁴ erywhere, with all gratitude. ·I do not want to take up too much of your time, but I beg you to ⁵ give us a brief hearing. ·The plain truth is that we find this man a perfect pest; he stirs up trouble among Jews the world over, and is a ringleader of ⁶ the Nazarene sect. ·He has even attempted to pro- fane the Temple. We placed him under arrest, in- ⁷ tending to judge him according to our Law, ·but the tribune Lysias intervened and took him out of ⁸ our hands by force, ·ordering his accusers to ap- pear before you; if you ask him you can find out for yourself the truth of all our accusations against ⁹ this man." ·The Jews supported him, asserting that these were the facts.

¹⁰ When the governor motioned him to speak, Paul answered:

"I know that you have administered justice over this nation for many years, and I can there- ¹¹ fore speak with confidence in my defense. ·As you can verify for yourself, it is no more than twelve days since I went up to Jerusalem on pil- ¹² grimage, ·and it is not true that they ever found me arguing with anyone or stirring up the mob, either in the Temple, in the synagogues, or about ¹³ the town; ·neither can they prove any of the accu- sations they are making against me now.

14 "What I do admit to you is this: it is according
to the Way which they describe as a sect that I
worship the God of my ancestors, retaining my
belief in all points of the Law and in what is writ-
15 ten in the prophets; ·and I hold the same hope in
God as they do that there will be a resurrection
16 of good men and bad men alike. ·In these things,
I, as much as they, do my best to keep a clear
conscience at all times before God and man.

17 "After several years I came to bring alms to
18 my nation and to make offerings; ·it was in connection with these that they found me in the
Temple; I had been purified, and there was no
19 crowd involved, and no disturbance. ·But some
Jews from Asia . . . —these are the ones who
should have appeared before you and accused me
20 of whatever they had against me. ·At least let
those who are present say what crime they found
me guilty of when I stood before the Sanhedrin,
21 unless it were to do with this single outburst,
when I stood up among them and called out: It
is about the resurrection of the dead that I am on
trial before you today."

22 At this Felix, who knew more about the Way
than most people, adjourned the case, saying,
"When Lysias the tribune has come down I will
23 go into your case." ·He then gave orders to the
centurion that Paul should be kept under arrest
but free from restriction, and that none of his
own people should be prevented from seeing to
his needs.

24 Some days later Felix came with his wife Dru-
silla who was a Jewess. He sent for Paul and gave
him a hearing on the subject of faith in Christ
25 Jesus. ·But when he began to treat of righteousness, self-control and the coming Judgment, Felix
took fright and said, "You may go for the present;
26 I will send for you when I find it convenient." ·At
the same time he had hopes of receiving money
from Paul, and for this reason he sent for him
frequently and had talks with him.

27 When the two years came to an end, Felix was

> succeeded by Porcius Festus and, being anxious
> to gain favor with the Jews, Felix left Paul in
> custody.

✠

In this section—act four of "Paul and the Jewish
Heritage"—Roman authority is front and center stage.
But before we can thoroughly appreciate the role the
Roman governor plays in this section, we must attend
to a technical problem, comparable to a problem with
stage lighting.

Verses 6b–8a are absent from the best Greek manu-
scripts of Acts, though the JB translation, seeking to
give its readers more information about Paul's trial, has
kept them. Actually, this part of Tertullus' brilliant ora-
tory should go: "He has even attempted to profane the
Temple. We placed him under arrest. If you ask him
[that is, Paul], you can find out for yourself the truth of
all our accusations against him."

Now that we have resolved this technical problem, we
can direct our full attention to Felix, the Roman governor. Imagine him in the center of the stage on his judgment seat. The prosecution is to his right, the accused
to his left. Both the Jews and Paul defer to his power.
Such deference is reflected in the ingratiating remarks of
24:2–4, 10b. After Tertullus has completed his brief
and the Jews have witnessed to its veracity, Felix does
not utter a sound but authoritatively nods to Paul to
defend himself. After both parties have aired their posi-
tions, Felix pronounces one of the two lines assigned to
him in this act: "When Lysias the tribune has come
down I will go into your case" (24:22). Felix does not
need long speeches to convince people of his power; he
emanates power. Luke's purpose in staging act four this
way is to highlight Paul's innocence (see also 23:29;

25:18-19; 26:31-32). Felix has heard the case according to protocol and has not condemned Paul. But verses 24-27, which form a brief scene at the end of act four, reveal another side of Felix's character. He is greedy (24:26) and keeps Paul in detention to please the Jews (24:27). This view of Felix accords with the portrait painted by the Roman historian Tacitus: Felix "wielded the power of a king with all the instincts of a slave." (*Histories* 5, 9, Loeb translation). Luke may be intent on showing that Roman authorities are fair in judging cases involving Christians, but he is not blind to the shady side of the exercise of power (see the commentary on 16:11-40).

The Jews act according to character in this section. Their accusation in 24:5 would be more forceful if "stirs up trouble" were more literally translated as "incites riots." This accusation is meant to give Felix the impression that Paul is involved in *sedition*. It should be noted that the accusations in 24:5-6 are echoes of Luke 23:2: "They began their accusation [against Jesus] by saying, 'We found this man inciting our people to revolt, opposing payment of the tribute to Caesar, and claiming to be Christ, a king.'" This is another instance in which Paul's life is parallel to Jesus'.

Paul's defense powerfully answers the allegation leveled against him (see 21:28). We can fathom Luke's purpose for this apology by noticing that Paul does not explicitly mention Jesus Christ. Paul, the pious Jew, brings alms, makes offerings, and is purified in the Temple. He is not involved in sedition. In following the way of God (that is, Christianity), Paul does not deny but actually affirms his Jewish heritage (24:14-16). In becoming a Christian and a Christian missionary, Paul has remained faithful to his Pharisaic heritage of belief in the resurrection of the dead (24:21; see 23:6). Attacked by Jews and Jewish Christians because of their

fidelity to Paul, Luke's communities draw strength from
Paul's sterling defense of his Jewish heritage.

STUDY QUESTION: In Felix the age-old story of power
and innocence is played out. Does
power corrupt?

¹ **25** Three days after his arrival in the province, Festus went up to Jerusalem from Caesarea. ² The chief priests and leaders of the Jews informed ³ him of the case against Paul, urgently ·asking him to support them rather than Paul, and to have him transferred to Jerusalem. They were, in fact, pre- ⁴ paring an ambush to murder him on the way. ·But Festus replied that Paul would remain in custody in Caesarea, and that he would be going back ⁵ there shortly himself. ·"Let your authorities come down with me," he said, "and if there is anything wrong about the man, they can bring a charge against him."

⁶ After staying with them for eight or ten days at the most, he went down to Caesarea and the next day he took his seat on the tribunal and had ⁷ Paul brought in. ·As soon as Paul appeared, the Jews who had come down from Jerusalem sur- rounded him, making many serious accusations ⁸ which they were unable to substantiate. ·Paul's defense was this, "I have committed no offense whatever against either Jewish law, or the Tem- ⁹ ple, or Caesar." ·Festus was anxious to gain favor with the Jews, so he said to Paul, "Are you will- ing to go up to Jerusalem and be tried on these ¹⁰ charges before me there?" ·But Paul replied, "I am standing before the tribunal of Caesar and this is where I should be tried. I have done the ¹¹ Jews no wrong, as you very well know. ·If I am guilty of committing any capital crime, I do not ask to be spared the death penalty. But if there is no substance in the accusations these persons bring against me, no one has a right to surrender ¹² me to them. I appeal to Caesar." ·Then Festus conferred with his advisers and replied, "You

have appealed to Caesar; to Caesar you shall go."

13 Some days later King Agrippa and Bernice arrived in Caesarea and paid their respects to Festus.
14 Their visit lasted several days, and Festus put Paul's case before the king. "There is a man here," he said, "whom Felix left behind in cus-
15 tody, ·and while I was in Jerusalem the chief priests and elders of the Jews laid information
16 against him, demanding his condemnation. ·But I told them that Romans are not in the habit of surrendering any man, until the accused confronts his accusers and is given an opportunity to
17 defend himself against the charge. ·So they came here with me, and I wasted no time but took my seat on the tribunal the very next day and had
18 the man brought in. ·When confronted with him, his accusers did not charge him with any of the
19 crimes I had expected; ·but they had some argument or other with him about their own religion and about a dead man called Jesus whom Paul
20 alleged to be alive. ·Not feeling qualified to deal with questions of this sort, I asked him if he would be willing to go to Jerusalem to be tried
21 there on this issue. ·But Paul put in an appeal for his case to be reserved for the judgment of the august emperor, so I ordered him to be remanded
22 until I could send him to Caesar." ·Agrippa said to Festus, "I should like to hear the man myself." "Tomorrow," he answered, "you shall hear him."

23 So the next day Agrippa and Bernice arrived in great state and entered the audience chamber attended by the tribunes and the city notables;
24 and Festus ordered Paul to be brought in. ·Then Festus said, "King Agrippa, and all here present with us, you see before you the man about whom the whole Jewish community has petitioned me, both in Jerusalem and here, loudly protesting that
25 he ought not to be allowed to remain alive. ·For my own part I am satisfied that he has committed no capital crime, but when he himself appealed to the august emperor I decided to send him.
26 But I have nothing definite that I can write to his Imperial Majesty about him; that is why I have

produced him before you all, and before you in particular, King Agrippa, so that after the exami- 27 nation I may have something to write. ·It seems to me pointless to send a prisoner without indicating the charges against him."

✠

At first glance this section—act five of "Paul and the Jewish Heritage"—is like an auto caught in the stranglehold of snow. There is frantic spinning of wheels, but no movement forward. It seems that Luke serves up the same menu again: Jewish accusations, Paul's defense, and Roman certification of innocence. But as often is the case, first impressions are deceptive. With "You have appealed to Caesar; to Caesar you shall go" (25:12), the play and Acts have taken a gargantuan step forward. Paul is on his way to Rome—to Caesar, to the august emperor (25:21), to his Imperial Majesty (25:26). This appeal fulfills Jesus' words: "Courage! You have *borne witness* for me in Jerusalem, now you must do the same in Rome" (23:11). The stage is set for chapter 26 and the sixth and final act. The way is prepared for the denouement of Acts when Paul's arrival in Rome (chapter 28) fulfills Jesus' words: "you will be my *witnesses* not only in Jerusalem but throughout Judaea and Samaria, and indeed to the ends of the earth" (1:8).

In the space remaining we dedicate a few lines to each of the main characters. First, the Jews. Luke varies his description of them, but most often uses a term which means "religious leaders" (see 25:2, 5, 7, 15, 24). They are intent on ridding the earth of Paul either by ambush (25:3) or by Roman condemnation to death (25:15).

Paul is innocent of capital charges and has committed no offense either against Jewish Law or the Temple (25:8–11, 18–19, 25). In his appearance before a

Roman governor (Festus) and a king (Agrippa) he is
likened once more to Jesus (see Lk 23:6–12). Festus'
repeated acknowledgment of Paul's innocence is similar to that of Pilate at Jesus' trial (see Lk 23:4,
14–15, 22). Paul's appearance before a governor and a
king also recalls Luke 21:12–13: "But before all this
happens, men will seize you and persecute you; they
will hand you over to the synagogues and to imprisonment, and bring you before kings and governors because of my name—and that will be your opportunity *to
bear witness.*"

Festus, the Roman governor, is the epitome of the
efficient and just ruler: "So they came here with me,
and I wasted no time but took my seat on the tribunal
the very next day and had the man brought in"
(25:17). And since this model public servant can dis-
cover nothing worthy of death in Paul's conduct, how
can Christianity be a seditious movement in the Roman
Empire? So it is crystal clear that Festus is a finely
tuned official. But what is murky is the entire appeal
scene (25:11–12). Luke describes Festus as allowing
Paul to appeal a decision which Festus himself never
pronounced. Put another way, if Paul had been condemned, he could have appealed that verdict. But he
appeals a verdict which was never pronounced. It
seems best to resolve this problem by conjecturing that
Luke knew that Paul had appealed to Caesar. He didn't
know the what or the why. Ignorant of the complexities
of the appeal procedures, he constructs his story
around the fact of Paul's appeal. Luke's purpose in
writing Acts is to edify his communities, not to promul-
gate the minutes of court trials.

STUDY QUESTION: In the flow of Luke's story and
                theology why was it so important
                that Paul journey to Rome?

THE CHRISTIAN MISSION AND THE JEWS

1 **26** Then Agrippa said to Paul, "You have leave to speak on your own behalf." And Paul held up his hand and began his defense:

2 "I consider myself fortunate, King Agrippa, in that it is before you I am to answer today all the 3 charges made against me by the Jews, ·the more so because you are an expert in matters of custom and controversy among the Jews. So I beg you to listen to me patiently.

4 "My manner of life from my youth, a life spent from the beginning among my own people and in Jerusalem, is common knowledge among the Jews. 5 They have known me for a long time and could testify, if they would, that I followed the strictest 6 party in our religion and lived as a Pharisee. ·And now it is for my hope in the promise made by 7 God to our ancestors that I am on trial, ·the promise that our twelve tribes, constant in worship night and day, hope to attain. For that hope, 8 Sire, I am actually put on trial by Jews! ·Why does it seem incredible to you that God should raise the dead?

9 "As for me, I once thought it was my duty to use every means to oppose the name of Jesus the 10 Nazarene. ·This I did in Jerusalem; I myself threw many of the saints into prison, acting on authority from the chief priests, and when they were sen- 11 tenced to death I cast my vote against them. ·I often went around the synagogues inflicting penalties, trying in this way to force them to renounce their faith; my fury against them was so extreme that I even pursued them into foreign cities.

12 "On one such expedition I was going to Damascus, armed with full powers and a commis-

¹³ sion from the chief priests, ·and at midday as I
was on my way, your Majesty, I saw a light
brighter than the sun come down from heaven.
It shone brilliantly around me and my fellow
¹⁴ travelers. ·We all fell to the ground, and I heard
a voice saying to me in Hebrew, 'Saul, Saul, why
are you persecuting me? It is hard for you, kick-
¹⁵ ing like this against the goad.' ·Then I said: Who
are you, Lord? And the Lord answered, 'I am Je-
¹⁶ sus, and you are persecuting me. ·But get up and
stand on your feet, for I have appeared to you for
this reason: to appoint you as my servant and as
witness of this vision in which you have seen me,
¹⁷ and of others in which I shall appear to you. ·I
shall deliver you from the people and from the
¹⁸ pagans, to whom I am sending you ·to open their
eyes, so that they may turn from darkness to light,
from the dominion of Satan to God, and receive,
through faith in me, forgiveness of their sins and
a share in the inheritance of the sanctified.'

¹⁹   "After that, King Agrippa, I could not disobey
²⁰ the heavenly vision. ·On the contrary I started
preaching first to the people of Damascus, then
to those of Jerusalem and all the countryside of
Judaea, and also to the pagans, urging them to
repent and turn to God, proving their change of
²¹ heart by their deeds. ·This was why the Jews laid
hands on me in the Temple and tried to do away
²² with me. ·But I was blessed with God's help, and
so I have stood firm to this day, testifying to
great and small alike, saying nothing more than
what the prophets and Moses himself said would
²³ happen: ·that the Christ was to suffer and that, as
the first to rise from the dead, he was to proclaim
that light now shone for our people and for the
pagans too."

²⁴   He had reached this point in his defense when
Festus shouted out, "Paul, you are out of your
mind; all that learning of yours is driving you
²⁵ mad." ·"Festus, your Excellency," answered Paul,
"I am not mad: I am speaking nothing but the
²⁶ sober truth. ·The king understands these matters,
and to him I now speak with assurance, confident

that nothing of all this is lost on him; after all,
27 these things were not done in a corner. ·King
Agrippa, do you believe in the prophets? I know
28 you do." ·At this Agrippa said to Paul, "A little
more, and your arguments would make a Chris-
29 tian of me." ·"Little or more," Paul replied, "I
wish before God that not only you but all who
have heard me today would come to be as I am
—except for these chains."
30   At this the king rose to his feet, with the governor and Bernice and those who sat there with
31 them. ·When they had retired they talked together
and agreed, "This man is doing nothing that de-
32 serves death or imprisonment." ·And Agrippa remarked to Festus, "The man could have been set
free if he had not appealed to Caesar."

✟

Imagine that this section rings the curtain down on
"Paul and the Jewish Heritage" and that we are eaves-
dropping on four students rapping about the meaning
of the play. Their comments jog one another's memories; the acuteness of one's observations gives birth to
the insights of another.

Al opens the discussion and calls the group's attention to how the playwright repeatedly stresses the
Roman declaration of Paul's innocence. "Why, see,
how important this theme is. The last lines of the play
pulse with its blood: 'This man is doing nothing that
deserves death or imprisonment. . . . The man could
have been set free if he had not appealed to Caesar.'"
All eyes are on Al as he momentarily pauses, gulps a
breath, and continues: "How wise the Romans are!
Luke portrays them as shrewd enough to see that Jewish accusations of Christians concern matters of religion and not matters in which the Roman authorities
have competence. Small wonder that Festus thought
Paul was mad when he said that the prophets testify

that Christ would rise from the dead. Those Romans are sure smart!" Happy with the points he has made, Al glances around the table for approval and likes what he sees.

After a polite pause, Theresa, animated as usual, cracks the silence wide open with: "You know, Agrippa's a Jew!"

"Terri, you've stated the obvious. What are you after?" Al half teases.

Terri resumes: "I was getting sort of bored with Paul when he went into his call for the third time. I began to note some inconsistencies in his story and followed them to keep myself awake. I was picking up bits and pieces when all of a sudden Agrippa's words caused the entire jigsaw puzzle to fall into place: 'A little more, and your arguments would make a Christian of me.' You may think I'm way off base, but I think that Luke uses this account of Paul's call as a way of converting Jews to Christianity."

"What do you mean?" asks Harry.

"Doesn't it strike you as odd that Paul doesn't answer the accusations of speaking against Moses, etc. He seems to be arguing that Christianity fulfills the Jewish hopes and scriptures. I can't help but think that when Paul says, 'Why does it seem incredible to you that God should raise the dead?' that he is referring to Jews of Luke's time who find fault with Christians, especially those of a Pauline persuasion. I don't know. Let me think about this some more. Any of you got any ideas on this?"

Harry, a veteran and graying with wisdom, affirms Terri: "Terri, your remarks make a lot of sense to me. During the entire play I have been identifying with Paul. In this final act Luke has pitched the character of Paul to make the very points you suggested."

"Wow, that's great! How does he do it?" Terri exclaims.

Harry clears his throat, cradles his pipe in his right hand, gazes at Terri and says, "Luke has often told us that Paul was a pious Jew, a Pharisee, etc. There's a line in this act which sticks in my mind: 'As for me, I once thought it was my duty to use every means to oppose the name of Jesus the Nazarene.' That's a new line for Paul and seems specially constructed by Luke to win over those who at one time may have thought and felt the same way Paul did. Paul would never have changed his stance were it not for God's call. His mission to the pagans was God's choice, not his. Why, if it weren't for the Lord's call, strong-willed Paul would probably still be there on the road to Damascus uselessly trying to kick against the prod. Terri, I agree with you wholeheartedly."

Terri was very pleased with Harry's observations. Al beamed his approval at both. The silence became loud, and all three looked in Connie's direction.

Connie was the quiet type, who warmed to ideas slowly. Once she became comfortable with them, sparks of insight flashed in all directions. "You know, guys," she almost whispered, "the image that surfaces in my mind is that of a play within a play. Terri, you triggered this insight in my mind when you referred to Luke's first two narrations of Paul's call. I began to think that Luke may be drawing on themes from his larger play of Acts for this play of chapters 21 to 26. Three points dawned on me. Number one: When Paul told Festus, 'These things were not done in a corner,' I couldn't help but think of how public the Christian proclamation has been in the story of Acts. The apostles preach to thousands in Jerusalem. Paul preaches before the Roman governor, Sergius Paulus, etc. Al, this point agrees with the one you made so well. Christianity is not an underground movement bent on creating dissension and sedition in the Roman Empire. What it does, it does in broad daylight."

"Thanks, Connie, that's a fine observation," Al remarked.

Connie continued: "My second point is that throughout Acts Luke has been concerned with the issue of persecution. In this final act Paul jokes about his chains and assures those who follow in his footsteps that the Lord rescues from persecution. Remember Paul's lines: 'I shall deliver you from the people and from the pagans' and 'But I was blessed with God's help, and so I have stood firm to this day.' With God on his side, what do Paul and those missionaries who imitate him have to fear? Harry, my third point is a confirmation of some of your observations. These past days I have been studying how God called the prophets. These call stories have made such a strong impression on me that I memorized them. I was amazed when I heard Paul use them in his story of how the Lord called him. I know it's getting late, so I'll just quote one passage from the prophet Jeremiah: 'I have appointed you as a prophet to the nations. . . . Go now to those to whom I send you and say whatever I command you. Do not be afraid of them, for I am with you to protect you' (1:5, 7–8). Harry, I would piggyback on your insight this way. Luke has taken great pains to accentuate the theme that God fulfills his promises. At times this theme can float off to the ninth level of abstraction. In Paul Luke has found a concrete example of how God has fulfilled his promises. By the very fact that Paul has gone to the nations he is the living embodiment of the truth that God does fulfill his promises. In this case, the promise that the pagans would worship Israel's God—the God who raised Jesus from the dead. I agree with

what you've all said. You've helped me to appreciate
some of the depth of this play. Thanks."

Connie's observations capped the discussion, but not
the pondering of these four theatergoers. "Paul and the
Jewish Heritage" was one of the most powerful plays
they had seen in years.

STUDY QUESTIONS: Is "Paul and the Jewish Heritage"
Luke's way of converting Pharisee
Jews to Christianity? Is it his way
of providing his communities with
arguments against Jews who harass
Christian missionaries? Is it his
way of consoling his communities
that the Roman authorities are
just? Is it all of the above, none of
the above, or what?

THE INNOCENT PAUL BRINGS SALVATION

1 **27** When it had been decided that we should sail for Italy, Paul and some other prisoners were handed over to a centurion called Julius, of
2 the Augustan cohort. ·We boarded a vessel from Adramyttium bound for ports on the Asiatic coast, and put to sea; we had Aristarchus with us,
3 a Macedonian of Thessalonika. ·Next day we put in at Sidon, and Julius was considerate enough to allow Paul to go to his friends to be looked after.
4 From there we put to sea again, but as the winds were against us we sailed under the lee of
5 Cyprus, ·then across the open sea off Cilicia and Pamphylia, taking a fortnight to reach Myra in
6 Lycia. ·There the centurion found an Alexandrian ship leaving for Italy and put us aboard.
7 For some days we made little headway, and we had difficulty in making Cnidus. The wind would not allow us to touch there, so we sailed under the
8 lee of Crete off Cape Salmone ·and struggled along the coast until we came to a place called Fair Havens, near the town of Lasea.
9 A great deal of time had been lost, and navigation was already hazardous since it was now well after the time of the Fast, so Paul gave them this
10 warning, ·"Friends, I can see this voyage will be dangerous and that we run the risk of losing not only the cargo and the ship but also our lives as
11 well." ·But the centurion took more notice of the captain and the ship's owner than of what Paul
12 was saying; ·and since the harbor was unsuitable for wintering, the majority were for putting out from there in the hope of wintering at Phoenix—a harbor in Crete, facing southwest and northwest.

13   A southerly breeze sprang up and, thinking their
objective as good as reached, they weighed anchor
14 and began to sail past Crete, close inshore. ·But it
was not long before a hurricane, the "northeaster"
as they call it, burst on them from across the is-
15 land. ·The ship was caught and could not be turned
head on to the wind, so we had to give way to it
16 and let ourselves be driven. ·We ran under the lee
of a small island called Cauda and managed with
some difficulty to bring the ship's boat under con-
17 trol. ·They hoisted it aboard and with the help of
tackle bound cables around the ship; then, afraid
of running aground on the Syrtis banks, they
floated out the sea anchor and so let themselves
18 drift. ·As we were making very heavy weather of
it, the next day they began to jettison the cargo,
19 and the third day they threw the ship's gear over-
20 board with their own hands. ·For a number of
days both the sun and the stars were invisible and
the storm raged unabated until at last we gave up
all hope of surviving.

21   Then, when they had been without food for
a long time, Paul stood up among the men.
"Friends," he said, "if you had listened to me
and not put out from Crete, you would have
22 spared yourselves all this damage and loss. ·But
now I ask you not to give way to despair. There
23 will be no loss of life at all, only of the ship. ·Last
night there was standing beside me an angel of
24 the God to whom I belong and whom I serve, ·and
he said, 'Do not be afraid, Paul. You are destined
to appear before Caesar, and for this reason God
grants you the safety of all who are sailing with
25 you.' ·So take courage, friends; I trust in God
26 that things will ·turn out just as I was told; but
we are to be stranded on some island."

27   On the fourteenth night we were being driven
one way and another in the Adriatic, when about
midnight the crew sensed that land of some sort
28 was near. ·They took soundings and found twenty
fathoms; after a short interval they sounded again
29 and found fifteen fathoms. ·Then, afraid that we
might run aground somewhere on a reef, they

dropped four anchors from the stern and prayed
30 for daylight. ·When some of the crew tried to escape from the ship and lowered the ship's boat
into the sea as though to lay out anchors from the
31 bows, ·Paul said to the centurion and his men,
"Unless those men stay on board you cannot hope
32 to be saved." ·So the soldiers cut the boat's ropes
and let it drop away.

33 Just before daybreak Paul urged them all to
have something to eat. "For fourteen days," he
said, "you have been in suspense, going hungry
34 and eating nothing. ·Let me persuade you to have
something to eat; your safety is not in doubt. Not
35 a hair of your heads will be lost." ·With these
words he took some bread, gave thanks to God
in front of them all, broke it and began to eat.
36 Then they all plucked up courage and took
37 something to eat themselves. ·We were in all two
hundred and seventy-six souls on board that ship.
38 When they had eaten what they wanted they light-
ened the ship by throwing the corn overboard
into the sea.

39 When day came they did not recognize the land,
but they could make out a kind of bay with a
beach; they planned to run the ship aground on
40 this if they could. ·They slipped the anchors and
left them to the sea, and at the same time loosened
the lashings of the rudders; then, hoisting the
foresail to the wind, they headed for the beach.
41 But the crosscurrents carried them into a shoal
and the vessel ran aground. The bows were
wedged in and stuck fast, while the stern began
to break up with the pounding of the waves.

42 The soldiers planned to kill the prisoners for
43 fear that any should swim off and escape. ·But
the centurion was determined to bring Paul safely
through, and would not let them do what they in-
tended. He gave orders that those who could swim
44 should jump overboard first and so get ashore, ·and
the rest follow either on planks or on pieces of
wreckage. In this way all came safe and sound to
land.

¹ **28** Once we had come safely through, we discovered that the island was called Malta.
² The inhabitants treated us with unusual kindness. They made us all welcome, and they lit a huge fire because it had started to rain and the weather was
³ cold. ·Paul had collected a bundle of sticks and was putting them on the fire when a viper brought
⁴ out by the heat attached itself to his hand. ·When the natives saw the creature hanging from his hand they said to one another, "That man must be a murderer; he may have escaped the sea, but
⁵ divine vengeance would not let him live." ·However, he shook the creature off into the fire and
⁶ came to no harm, ·although they were expecting him at any moment to swell up or drop dead on the spot. After they had waited a long time without seeing anything out of the ordinary happen to him, they changed their minds and began to say he was a god.

⁷ In that neighborhood there were estates belonging to the prefect of the island, whose name was Publius. He received us and entertained us hos-
⁸ pitably for three days. ·It so happened that Publius' father was in bed, suffering from feverish attacks and dysentery. Paul went in to see him, and after a prayer he laid his hands on the man and
⁹ healed him. ·When this happened, the other sick people on the island came as well and were cured;
¹⁰ they honored us with many marks of respect, and when we sailed they put on board the provisions we needed.

¹¹ At the end of three months we set sail in a ship that had wintered in the island; she came from Alexandria and her figurehead was the
¹² Twins. ·We put in at Syracuse and spent three
¹³ days there; ·from there we followed the coast up to Rhegium. After one day there a south wind sprang up and on the second day we made Puteoli,
¹⁴ where we found some brothers and were much rewarded by staying a week with them. And so we came to Rome.

¹⁵ When the brothers there heard of our arrival

they came to meet us, as far as the Forum of
Appius and the Three Taverns. When Paul saw
16 them he thanked God and took courage. ·On our
arrival in Rome Paul was allowed to stay in lodg-
ings of his own with the soldier who guarded him.

✠

Four points pulsate through this long and exciting
section: (1) the motif of the storm at sea; (2) Luke's
modifications of this motif by Paul's speeches; (3)
Luke's folklore proof of Paul's innocence; (4) Paul's
arrival in Rome.

The motif of the storm at sea. We are so fortunate
today to have smooth, safe, and efficient travel by ship,
plane, train, and car that we rarely think back to earlier
days and the hazards of travel. In the case at hand, we
can begin to appreciate some of the hazards of travel
by sea by recalling Paul's words: "Three times I have
been shipwrecked and once adrift in the open sea for a
night and a day" (2 Co 11:25). Paul's almost noncha-
lant description sends shivers up our spines. Because
travel by sea was so hazardous it quickly became a
multipurpose motif. In his *The Ship; or, the Wishes*
Lucian of Samosata tells about a violent storm at sea:
"Then, having now lost their course, they sailed across
the Aegean beating up with the trade winds against
them, and yesterday, seventy days after leaving Egypt,
they anchored in Piraeus, after being driven so far
downwind. . . . Upon my word, that's an amazing pilot
you speak of, this Heron, as old as Nereus, who went
so far astray" (paragraphs 9–10, Loeb translation).
Lucian uses the motif of the storm at sea to show the
prowess of the pilot.

In another work, *Toxaris; or, Friendship,* Lucian
tells of a man who had fallen overboard in a storm:
"Think now, in the name of the gods! What firmer

proof of affection could a man display towards a friend who had fallen overboard at night into a sea so wild, than that of sharing his death? I beg you, envisage the tumult of the seas, the roar of the breaking water, the boiling spume, the night, the despair; then one man strangling, barely keeping up his head, holding his arms out to his friend, and other leaping after him at once, swimming with him, fearing that Damon would perish first" (paragraph 20, Loeb translation). The motif of the storm at sea becomes a means of demonstrating the bonds of friendship.

In the biblical story of Jonah the storm at sea illustrates something quite different. The storm is caused by Jonah's sin against Yahweh. As Jonah moans: "Take me and throw me into the sea, and then it will grow calm for you. For I can see it is my fault this violent storm has happened to you" (1:12). Jonah's entreaties win over his shipmates: "And taking hold of Jonah they threw him into the sea; and the sea grew calm again" (1:15). Jonah was polluted by his sin of disobedience and contaminated all who came into contact with him. All in the ship with Jonah shared his punishment.

Thus, we can see that the motif of a storm at sea was a common one at the time that Luke wrote. Let us see now how he used that motif.

Paul's speeches and the motif of the storm at sea. Luke has modified the motif by putting small speeches into Paul's mouth. A study of the vocabulary of the speeches would indicate that they are composed by Luke. Also it is implausible that Paul would be able or allowed to give these speeches. Consider, for example, that Paul, a chained prisoner, would have to scream, while "the storm raged unabated," in a voice loud enough that all 276 people could hear him

(27:21–26). Even if he had a megaphone, no one
would hear him.

If we peer intently at the content of Paul's speeches,
we can spot ways in which Luke has used the motif of
a storm at sea. Paul's one-sentence speech in 27:10 has
the effect of underlining Paul's status as a spokesman
for God—Paul prophesies. Because Paul is destined to
appear before Caesar, God grants him "the safety of all
who are sailing" with him (27:21–26). Thus on one
level, Paul is a means of physical salvation for all these
people. But Luke implies a deeper meaning: Paul, the
missionary-preacher, is God's instrument of salvation
for all peoples. Paul's final speech in 27:31–38 is ex-
ceedingly strange. With words reminiscent of eucharistic passages, Luke writes: "With these words he took
some bread, gave thanks to God in front of them all,
broke it and began to eat" (27:35, see Lk 9:16;
22:19; 24:30; Ac 20:11). It is patent that Luke is
using eucharistic terminology, but it is just as clear that
Paul is not celebrating a Eucharist for his pagan shipmates. It seems that Luke uses the example of Paul's
meal to prompt his Christian readers to recall their experience of the breaking of the eucharistic bread when
they, like Paul, are in dire straits. The Lord who is present at Eucharist will save his community from harassment just as he delivered Paul from the storm at sea. In
sum, Luke is able to console his community, tossed by
the waters of persecution, by directing their gaze at
their missionary hero Paul and at their Savior present
in the breaking of bread.

Luke's folklore proof of Paul's innocence. At earlier
points in this commentary (e.g., 5:12–16) we cau-
tioned that Luke is not above employing what we
would call folklore motifs to convey his message. This
section provides us with further examples. The key passages are these: "In this way all came safe and sound

to land" (27:44). "That man must be a murderer; he
may have escaped the sea, but divine vengeance would
not let him live. . . . they changed their minds and
began to say he was a god" (28:4–6). "And after a
prayer he (Paul) laid his hands on the man and healed
him. When this happened, the other sick people on the
island came as well and were cured" (28:8–9). In
ways that communicated a powerful message, Luke is
saying that God has vindicated Paul of all accusations
of guilt. Paul is innocent. Paul is not another Jonah
who, polluted by crime, causes the storm at sea. In
Paul's case all came safe and sound to land. The inhabitants of Malta know nothing about Paul, especially
about his speeches on board ship, and interpret his
snake bite as a sure sign that he is a murderer. He
might have escaped the storm at sea, but divine vengeance caught up with him on land. They are mistaken.
Paul is innocent. The miracles which Paul performs—
notice that Paul does not preach the gospel to the natives—are further confirmation from God that Paul is
innocent. Using the language of folklore, Luke projects
these huge letters in the sky over Rome: PAUL IS INNO-
CENT. Since God has attested Paul's innocence in such
a majestic way, it would be anticlimactic for Luke to
portray Paul pleading his case before Caesar (27:24
indicates that Luke knew that Paul did actually appear
before Caesar).

Paul's arrival in Rome. Acts 28:11–16 describes
Paul's arrival in Rome. Paul fulfills Jesus' promise of
1:8 (see also 19:21 and 23:11). Rome is "the ends of
the earth." Luke wants to give the impression that Paul
is also the great missionary to Rome. Notice how he
refers to the Christians in Rome simply as "brothers."
He does not refer to any churches (28:14–15). This
odd way of writing about the Christians in Rome is
paralleled in Acts 19:1–10, where Luke mentions that

there were disciples in Ephesus before Paul arrived
(19:1–7). But these drop completely out of the picture
in the narration of 19:8–10. Luke is desirous of paint-
ing Paul as the founder of the church at Ephesus—and
of the church at Rome.

Luke has used the motif of the storm at sea to make
some telling points for his communities. By preserving
him from the storm, the shipwreck, and the snake, God
has pronounced a verdict of innocent over Paul. The
God in whom the persecuted Paul trusted is the same
God who is present at the breaking of bread within
Luke's communities. In the person of the great missionary Paul, the gospel has arrived in Rome.

STUDY QUESTIONS: In what way does a contemporary
Christian experience salvation at
the Eucharist? Does Luke fail to
mention that Paul evangelized
Malta? Why has the Roman centurion Julius taken a back seat to
Paul in this section? Julius was in
charge of the accused prisoner
Paul, wasn't he?

Acts 28:17-31
PAUL'S VISION OF MISSION

¹⁷ After three days he called together the leading Jews. When they had assembled, he said to them, "Brothers, although I have done nothing against our people or the customs of our ancestors, I was arrested in Jerusalem and handed over to the Ro-¹⁸ mans. ·They examined me and would have set me free, since they found me guilty of nothing in-¹⁹ volving the death penalty; ·but the Jews lodged an objection, and I was forced to appeal to Caesar, not that I had any accusation to make against my ²⁰ own nation. ·That is why I have asked to see you and talk to you, for it is on account of the hope of Israel that I wear this chain."

²¹ They answered, "We have received no letters from Judaea about you, nor has any countryman of yours arrived here with any report or story of ²² anything to your discredit. ·We think it would be as well to hear your own account of your position; all we know about this sect is that opinion everywhere condemns it."

²³ So they arranged a day with him and a large number of them visited him at his lodgings. He put his case to them, testifying to the kingdom of God and trying to persuade them about Jesus, arguing from the Law of Moses and the prophets. This went on from early morning until evening, ²⁴ and some were convinced by what he said, while ²⁵ the rest were skeptical. ·So they disagreed among themselves and, as they went away, Paul had one last thing to say to them, "How aptly the Holy Spirit spoke when he told your ancestors through the prophet Isaiah:

²⁶ Go to this nation and say:

You will hear and hear again but not under-
    stand,
see and see again, but not perceive.
27 For the heart of this nation has grown coarse,
their ears are dull of hearing and they have shut
    their eyes,
for fear they should see with their eyes,
hear with their ears,
understand with their heart,
and be converted
and be healed by me.

28 "Understand, then, that this salvation of God
has been sent to the pagans; they will listen to it."
30 Paul spent the whole of the two years in his
own rented lodging. He welcomed all who came
31 to visit him, ·proclaiming the kingdom of God
and teaching the truth about the Lord Jesus Christ
with complete freedom and without hindrance
from anyone.

✠

Recently I saw the movie *MacArthur*. All of us in
the theater knew that General Douglas MacArthur was
dead. The movie ended not with the details of his death
but with a powerful scene of the retired general
addressing the cadets at West Point. In that address
MacArthur summed up his views on life and thereby
bequeathed to these youths a vision of what dedicated
service to their country meant. This section is very similar to that last scene from *MacArthur*. Since Luke's
readers know of Paul's martyrdom in Rome, Luke opts
not to go into that point here. His purpose is not to
write chronicle history but to edify his readers. He presents Paul as the model missionary, who projects on the
screen of the future a moving vision of what mission is
all about. In what follows we sample the various components of that vision.

In chapters 21 to 26 Luke presented a six-act play, "Paul and the Jewish Heritage." Acts 28:17–20 is a brief summary of that play. Like Jesus, Paul "was handed over to the Romans." See Luke 24:7: "The Son of Man had to be handed over into the power of sinful men" (also see Ac 3:13). The Romans found Paul guilty of nothing involving the death penalty; Paul is innocent. Moreover, he has no accusation to make against his own nation. Paul stands in the best tradition of Judaism—Pharisaism. His very person argues that Christianity fulfills the hope of Israel. In these verses Luke announces the vision which this section will project. One of his main concerns in Acts has been to demonstrate that Christianity stands in firm continuity with Judaism.

Now that Luke has announced that the vision he bequeaths to his communities concerns the Jewish question, he explores a further facet of that vision in 28:21–22. Since the Christian mission had success among Jews and God-fearers, since Paul wrote an epistle to the Christians at Rome, and since Christians are mentioned in 28:14–15, one would expect that the Jews at Rome had previously met Christians. But that is not the Lukan view of things. For him, Paul is the first missionary to preach the Word to the Jews at Rome. It should be noted that the Jews are suspicious of the Christian mission: "All we know about this sect is that opinion everywhere condemns it" (28:22).

In 28:23–28 Luke opens up a broad avenue to his heart and mind and shares deeply his vision of the Jewish question. Paul begins his preaching in a new mission field by going to the Jews. He argues on the basis of the Law of Moses and the prophets and uses the traditional Jewish expectation of the kingdom of God to show that God's rule for salvation has been fulfilled in Jesus. Paul's quotation of Isaiah 6:9–10 in

28:26–27—contrary to a widespread opinion—does not
mean that the gentile Christians have slammed the door
of salvation in the Jews' face. As usually happened,
Paul converted some Jews: "some were convinced by
what he said" (28:24).

Three parallel passages in Acts help us appreciate
how Luke integrates Isaiah 6:9–10 into his vision of
the Jewish question. In 13:46 Paul and Barnabas speak
these stern words to the Jews at Pisidian Antioch: "We
had to proclaim the word of God to you first, but since
you have rejected it, since you do not think yourselves
worthy of eternal life, we must turn to the pagans." A
superficial reading of this passage might lead one to
think that Paul and Barnabas would never again cross
the threshold of a Jewish synagogue. Yet at their very
next mission at Iconium "they went to the Jewish synagogue, as they had at Antioch, and they spoke so effectively that a great many Jews and Greeks became
believers" (14:1). Paul uses a strong gesture and
words against the Jews in Corinth (18:6), but 18:8 reveals that his preaching in the Jewish synagogue there
did win over some Jews. Furthermore, Paul's next mission—to the Jews in Ephesus—shows that he has not
closed the book of salvation on the Jews (18:19).
Paul's mission at Ephesus provides such a striking parallel to 28:23–28 that it merits quotation in full:

He began by *going to the synagogue,* where
he spoke out boldly and argued persuasively
about the kingdom of God. He did this for three
months, till the attitude of some of the congregation *hardened into unbelief.* As soon as they began attacking the Way in front of the others, he
broke with them and took *his disciples* apart to
hold daily discussions in the lecture room of
Tyrannus. This went on for two years, with the

result that people from all over Asia, *both Jews
and Greeks,* were able to hear the word of the
Lord. [19:8–10]

The words which I have italicized demonstrate that
28:26–27 cannot be interpreted to mean that the
Christian mission has turned its back on the Jews. Paul
preaches to the Jews; some become disciples; some
harden their hearts; he preaches to all (see 28:30).

Since 28:26–27 is so vital for the interpretation of
Luke's purpose in writing Acts, let's approach these
problematic verses from still another perspective. Some
Jews believe (28:24); all Jews are blind (28:26–27).
How does one resolve this enigma? Behind the scenes
of these verses Luke struggles with the question of how
God fulfills his promises. Isaiah 6:9–10 is fulfilled in
Paul's preaching to the Jews at Rome; so is Acts 1:8,
because some Jews have believed; so is Psalm 67:2,
since the message of salvation goes to the pagans (see
28:28); and so is Luke 21:15, 18–19, since Paul
preaches safely and fearlessly. One cannot say that one
of these promises—e.g., Isaiah 6:9–10—is more important than another. At times there is tension, there is
mystery as God fulfills his promises in his own way. In
effect, Luke tells his communities that his vision of
Christian life and mission does not remove tension and
mystery. His communities should not pick and choose
among God's promises, but should allow God to be
God—a God who governs all things according to his
purpose and will. Luke also consoles his communities
with the realization that fulfillment of promise is not a
static reality. For example, the mere fact that the Lord
has fulfilled his missionary promise of 1:8 opens a door
to his intention: God is for mission. This vision of a
trustworthy God engenders new promises. The success
and safety of Paul the missionary gives a vision of hope

to Luke's missionary communities. God wills the success of their missionary activity and will be true to that purpose.

Acts 28:30–31 is not window dressing for the more important aspects of Luke's vision which preceded them. Paul welcomes all—both Jew and gentile. His preaching centers on the theme of Jesus, fulfillment of God's promise about his kingdom. The phrase "without hindrance from anyone" translates one Greek word which concludes Acts and literally means "unhindered." Some commentators have, with some reason, taken this final word of Luke's two-volume work as the key to its message. Luke has been striving might and main to show that the gospel message of salvation is unhindered—unhindered by class, religious, and economic distinctions. It is for outcast and well-bred, for Jew and gentile, for poor and rich. Also this message and those who carry it should not be hindered by Jews or by Romans. The Christian message is a valid outgrowth of Judaism, as the very existence of Paul the Pharisee and Christian loudly proclaims. The Christian message is not subversive; it presents no threat to Roman authority and peace. Luke also tells his missionaries that they should preach the message boldly although they may be hindered, like Paul, by imprisonment. Chains are incidental and should not stem the unhindered progress of the gospel.

In the person of the imprisoned Paul Luke summarizes his volume. His persecuted missionary communities are encouraged to continue their defense of how the Christian Way stands in harmonious continuity with Judaism. They should continue the difficult mission to the Jews. They should continue to preach the Word and not hinder anyone from accepting it. In the person of Paul, the model missionary, Luke presents his communities with a vision of what it means to be carriers of

God's Word. As with any vision of life, this vision is only validated by life—the life of Luke's communities and of those who follow in their missionary footsteps.

STUDY QUESTIONS: What does Luke's vision have to say to the church as it engages in missionary activity? Do contemporary churches hinder some people from accepting God's Word? When God fulfills a promise, does that mean that he is trustworthy and wills to fulfill other promises? In your own words, why did Luke write the Acts of the Apostles?

SUGGESTED FURTHER READINGS

Three studies will be of special help to the nonspecialist:

Keck, Leander E. *Mandate to Witness: Studies in the Book of Acts*. Valley Forge, Pa.: Judson, 1964. The major themes of Acts are treated from the perspective encapsuled in the book's title.

Lohfink, Gerhard. *The Conversion of St. Paul: Narrative and History in Acts*. Trans. and ed. Bruce J. Malina. Herald Scriptural Library. Chicago: Franciscan Herald, 1976. Lohfink explores the three accounts of Paul's call in Acts and discovers Luke's purpose in writing Acts.

Stagg, Frank. *The Book of Acts: The Early Struggle for an Unhindered Gospel*. Nashville: Broadman, 1955. The purpose of Acts is to plead that the Good News is open to all—Jew or gentile, outcast or well-bred, etc.

The following studies will aid the research of the advanced student:

Conzelmann, Hans. *The Theology of Saint Luke*. London: Faber and Faber, 1960. A groundbreaking work on Luke-Acts which propounds the view that the delay of the parousia is the occasion for Luke-Acts.

Dibelius, Martin. *Studies in the Acts of the Apostles*. Ed. Heinrich Greeven. London: SCM Press, 1956. A classic work, overflowing with insights.

Franklin, Eric. *Christ the Lord: A Study in the Purpose*

and Theology of Luke-Acts. Philadelphia: West-minster, 1975. A provocative study which excitingly probes the situation in which Luke authored his two-volume work.

Gasque, W. Ward. *A History of the Criticism of the Acts of the Apostles*. Grand Rapids, Mich.: Eerd-mans, 1975. Rich documentation, but overstresses the historical reliability of Acts.

Haenchen, Ernst. *The Acts of the Apostles: A Com-mentary*. Philadelphia: Westminster, 1971. A bril-liant commentary on Acts which rigorously asks and fruitfully answers the question of why Luke wrote Acts.

Jervell, Jacob. *Luke and the People of God: A New Look at Luke-Acts*. Minneapolis, Minn.: Augus-burg, 1972. A serious and convincing challenge to the dominant scholarly viewpoint that Christianity is the New Israel which replaces the old Israel.

Karris, Robert J. "Missionary Communities: A New Paradigm for the Study of Luke-Acts," *Catholic Bib-lical Quarterly* 40 (October 1978). This article pro-vides the scholarly underpinnings for the views espoused in this commentary and in its companion piece, *Invitation to Luke*.

Lampe, G. W. H. " 'Grievous wolves' (Acts 20:29)," in *Christ and Spirit in the New Testament,* ed. B. Lindars and S. S. Smalley, pp. 253–68. New York: Cambridge University Press, 1973. Develops the stimulating thesis that "in the late first and early sec-ond centuries the Church was faced with a powerful counterattack from the side of Judaism."